Wishing You the
BEST DAYs EVER!

BEST DAY EVER

Uncovering Your Strengths & Discovering Your Passion

Jessica Potts

BALSAM GLOW PUBLISHING

Cover Art by: Darren Booth
Design and Layout by: Brent Porter
Project Assistance by: Candy Ashbee
Edited by: Krystle Caputo
Proofread by: Paul Vance
With help from: Caren McTavish

Balsam Glow Publishing
Printed in Canada

ISBN (paperback): 978-1-7774112-0-6
ISBN (e-book): 978-1-7774112-1-3
ISBN (audiobook): 978-1-7774112-2-0

www.bestdayeverbook.com

Some names and identifying details have been changed to protect the privacy of individuals.

First Edition
10 9 8 7 6 5 4 3

For Domo, Lukey & Porter

The best of the best days are spent with you.

CONTENTS

Bonus resources and worksheets are available at: ***www.bestdayeverbook.com/bonus***

Why I wrote this book

It started with comments like "you're always smiling" and "I wish I could bottle your energy". When I started teaching at the post-secondary level, I found myself responding to students' questions about career and life advice with off-the-cuff, rich stories from my own experiences.

I jotted down these pivotal moments, and they translated well in other non-academic training sessions, webinars, retreats, and keynotes. So I started an inventory of stories and lessons and realized that there was a system others could easily follow that was relevant across ages and stages. Voilà!

I wrote this book after years of reflection, learning, and teaching. I've assisted hundreds of people in starting and growing their businesses. I've supported hundreds of students in launching their careers. And I've counselled and coached dozens of business leaders. There is a formula for success.

This book is for you:

- Whether you are a student or emerging leader at the start of your career looking to make the best choices or to accelerate your journey.
- Perhaps you are mid-career and looking to find meaning and purpose in what you are doing.
- Maybe you're an entrepreneur or budding entrepreneur who wants to take stock and take control.

- Perhaps you're at the top of your game and want to maintain the momentum.
- Or you're on your victory lap and looking to refocus.

How to use this book

You'll find 10 chapters in this book, each with stories, quotes, questions and exercises designed to help you live your best day ever every day. Each chapter builds on the last and also stands alone. That said, I recommend reading the chapters in order to build on each successive exercise. This book is also designed to address specific pain points, so you may wish to jump to a chapter or exercise that speaks to how you are feeling or evolving on your journey.

Along the way, I'll share some of my favourite stories from my own journey to offer social proof about how these methods have worked to shape me and help foster my own measure of success.

Simply put: success equals doing more of what you love.

That's not always an easy thing to figure out. So this book is designed to help you uncover your strengths and discover your passion through clarity, confidence, and courage.

But make no mistake, this book isn't for the person looking for a quick way to earn a big salary. This book is for the people who believe that while money isn't everything, it can be a byproduct of discovering your passion and confidently doing what you love.

"Without continuous personal growth, you are now all that you will ever be. And hell happens when the person you are meets the person you could have been."

- Eli Cohen

Prologue

'Imposter'

I met her - the person I could have been - over and over again. Feeling jealous, angry, lost, without purpose, lacking meaning, and worst of all, hopeless. I was continually comparing and trying to measure up to an impossible standard.

I've been in a place where I felt like there wasn't hope for a rewarding career and fruitful life, where complacency and comfort led me to the darkness.

Have you ever felt out of your league? I mean WAAAAAY out of your league? You somehow find yourself surrounded by seasoned veterans hitting home runs, and you feel like you're still hitting off the T-ball block? Have you ever heard that inner heckler's voice in your head,

"IMPOSTER.
IMPOSTER.
IMPOSTER."

Doubt starts to creep in. Maybe you feel discouraged,

overwhelmed, aimless, inadequate, or just stuck. It's exhausting and no way to live.

Have you ever found yourself asking, 'What makes me so special?' I have. It's the story of my life. Struggles and successes. Trials and triumphs. I've always rooted for the underdog because I am one. I haven't climbed Mount Everest. I haven't won an Olympic gold medal. I'm not an astronaut or Rhodes scholar, and I haven't swum with sharks.

But what I do have is contentment, happiness, and a deep sense of life satisfaction. I have clarity, confidence, courage, and my own measure of success and fulfilment. I love my life. I wake up excited. I feel passion and purpose. I feel valued and supported. I go to bed fulfilled.

So I've put together some simple strategies to allow each day to be your best day ever. That's a lofty statement, right? I mean, not every day can be your wedding day, or the birth of a child, or the day you get the big raise, or promotion, or partnership. I get that.

This book contains a collection of my stories threaded into life-changing questions, quotes, and reflection exercises to show you that living your best day ever, every day, is possible when we uncover our strengths and discover our passion.

Rewind

Since the lessons contained in this book come from my own

experiences, I think it's important to establish context. My beginnings are humble, my stumbles are numerous, my existence is flawed. That said, I've lived many lessons that have helped form my own measure of success.

Growing up, I was the underdog – nothing special. The only child of a single mom in small-town Ontario, Canada. A very quaint, white-picket-fence type of community. I was six-and-a-half when my parents split up, and my mom and I moved 6 hours away to the new town where we would start fresh. When my mom returned to her maiden name after the split, I became the only-of-my-name in a place where that type of thing mattered. I felt different, like an outsider. And I was always conscious of it.

My mom did her best. She worked hard and went without so I could feel like a normal kid – like I belonged. We didn't have a lot of money, but we did have a lot of love. Unfortunately, her best efforts didn't stop me from rebelling, and I was generally disengaged in high school. I may or may not have failed Grade 11 gym class.

Ok, I did.

I went away to college for a program called General Arts & Science. That's the program you take when you have no idea what you want to be when you grow up, but your mom won't let you take a year off to find yourself. She was scared that I would get a taste of the real world and never go to college at all.

I found my way to the business stream when I realized I needed to make a decision about switching programs to something more specialized. I had to commit, and I didn't feel ready.

"IMPOSTER.
IMPOSTER.
IMPOSTER."

The voice called again.

I had no idea as to what made me special, and that made this decision overwhelming. This would become a recurring pattern in my life and many of the lives of those around me.

I stopped by the school registrar's office, program guide in hand, pages dog-eared from where I had seen an area of mild interest. I sat nervously awaiting the next available staff member, looking for some guidance, advice, or a sign about the decision that would impact the rest of my life.

Then I overheard someone confidently, yet nonchalantly, talking about how she would be pursuing a dual diploma. Oooooh! A dual diploma, you say? It certainly caught my attention. This dual diploma she spoke of sounded so impressive. At that moment, I decided that I wanted to do that too. So with a clear goal in mind, that's what I did! In the exact two business fields of study that she had mentioned.

Can you see the flaw in this strategy? It was someone else's dream, but her confidence gave me the courage to get it done. Ironically, despite my best planning efforts, I fell two credits shy of achieving my prestigious dual diploma, but that's another story. It was the program I did graduate from where I felt a stronger connection. I was highly engaged with my coursework, classmates, and faculty.

I even managed to win a pair of awards at graduation. Me, a kid who felt wholly disengaged in high school, was graduating college with two awards! If I'm being frank, outside of an inspiring mentor, I wasn't sure how I had experienced this success. But there it was, and I wanted more.

It would take me years to figure out the formula for my own success and even longer to appreciate it. Here's what it boils down to:

Connect with yourself and understand your unique talents, values, skills, and experiences. Become fully aware of what makes you so special.

Connect with your context and understand how to align your talents, values, skills, and experiences with where you are and where you are going.

Connect with your goals and understand how to make an impact through meaningful, inspired action. It's time to live your dreams!

"Alignment with one's values eases the discomfort of growth."

- Jessica Potts

1.

Investing In Alignment

What makes me so special?

Chapter Purpose:

Regardless of our place in life, we are continually making decisions – big and small – that affect our path and our happiness. That can be scary and uncomfortable, but discomfort is also key to our personal growth.

This chapter's exercise is about establishing the foundation for your values and beliefs. With the safety net of knowing why you are doing it and how it contributes to your core values, you can confidently step outside your comfort zone.

Even better, clear values help attract the people, experiences, and opportunities you are naturally aligned with and repel the ones you aren't. Knowing your values will also allow you to recognize the difference so you can prioritize quickly and unapologetically.

Some people are blessed with knowing exactly what they want to be when they grow up. I was not one of those people. I was always envious of how easy everything seemed for those who had a clear path.

I had a friend in my teens who wanted to follow in her mother's footsteps of being a doctor. She grew up knowing the culture, rules, and steps to get there. Clear values were ingrained in her. She lived them. Many of her peers enjoyed an aimless summer of experimental drug use, but for this friend, abstinence came easy. She knew that the consequences of one night of fun could cost her the shot at her dream, so it was a hard no. We respected that.

Better still, her values naturally put distance between her and the people who could negatively influence and impact her goal. The icing on the cake was that she was simultaneously attracting the type of people who would have a positive impact by taking her stand. Her path was clear, values shared, decisions aligned, and she fast-tracked her education to become a decorated medical professional. I hear she's living happily ever after and on track to early retirement. Huzzah!

The rest of us have a lot of searching to do. Just like I did in college. I had no clear path and no real idea of what made me special or unique, so that made decision-making even more challenging. I chose the post-secondary institution that would launch me into the adult world and lead to gainful employment, all while ensuring that I found myself, for three main reasons. Two lame and one good:

1. I was accepted there. (Lame. I only applied to three places, each in cities where relatives had gone to school.)
2. I was afraid of big cities at the time. (Lame. I was limiting myself based on fear.)
3. It wasn't where my friends, or anyone I knew, were going, and this allowed a clean slate for personal growth. (Not lame.)

I had a good core circle of friends, many of whom went to the nearest college 30 minutes from home. But I needed to know who I would become outside of the small town where I felt like a disengaged underachiever, and 30 minutes was just too close.

I didn't feel like I belonged in that small town.

Even worse than my lack-lustre resume was being bright but not engaged. I felt like my life was set up to ensure that I couldn't reach my fullest potential (to any younger readers, that's the 90s way of saying 'living my best life'). In my modern-day lingo, I'd call it not being able to apply my talent in a meaningful way.

If only I could tell my younger self that when I channel genuine interest into something long enough to develop some skill, I will start to feel a sense of self-worth. Moving away represented a clean slate to discover who I was, not who other people said or inferred I was. I had a chip on my shoulder and something to prove. Still, purposely going to a place where I didn't know anyone at the tender age of 18 was venturing outside of my comfort zone.

I was going to learn the hard way, but it was my way.

This leap of faith ended well for me. But the problem is that we don't know enough about ourselves to make choices with any real degree of confidence in these critical decision-making years. Looking back at my decision-making criteria, I see the seeds of two of my core values around personal growth and family connection. But hindsight is MUCH easier than foresight, isn't it?

Fast forward to my second semester, and I was about to get way out of my comfort zone again. This time it was delivering my first formal verbal presentation as part of one of my classes. I can't recall the topic or even the teacher. What I do remember is the paralyzing fear coursing through my body. I was fighting to control my trembling hands and voice. A heatwave in my cheeks as my face turned a deep shade of red accompanied a mouth so dry my tongue stuck to the roof of it.

I received a 74% on that presentation and was utterly disappointed. It was a fair mark, and deep down, I knew it. I compared my effort to my classmate Kurt's, who had spent far less time preparing and seemed to be winging it with no visual aids, just sheer charm. Kurt got a mark well into the 80s.

Sure, Kurt was a more confident speaker - no doubt a product of his time spent doing missionary work and learning the art of conversation and confidence. But how did he make it look so effortless? It wasn't fair! I wanted to be instantly good at this and receive the accompanying validation of my teacher and peers.

As it turns out, growth is uncomfortable.

A year later, I started my senior year in the Marketing program. My cohorts had all gelled as we rallied behind a dynamic new professor and program coordinator who was shaking things up. His name was Les and he would become my first mentor outside of my mom. He hadn't been beaten down by the bureaucracy like so many others in tenured positions. His real-world experience, passion, and ideas made him different. Best of all, his dynamic classroom style and wisdom became part of our culture. Each class had a formal "thought for the day," a quote that blew our minds regularly and became the stuff of legends.

He taught a three-month course that included critiqued presentations with a different group of people every week. Looking back, I realize that the collaboration, problem-solving, presentation, and feedback giving/receiving taught me more than most other classes combined. By the end of the semester, I felt like I could present. I understood the mechanics of an excellent presentation and could deliver well with consistency. Yet still, I couldn't get comfortable with presenting. I would regularly get a jolt of adrenaline and occasionally get the red face if I didn't feel 1000% prepared.

Lingering after class one day late in the semester, Les and I chatted about how far the group had come. I confessed that no matter how many presentations I did, I still felt nervous leading up to it. My wise mentor looked at me and told me the most important words I had heard to date:

"YOU ARE ONLY NERVOUS BECAUSE YOU CARE."

- LES SMITH

These words were so impactful that some 20 years later, I still tell this story every week or two when counselling a friend, advising a client, or pep-talking a team member. You are only nervous because you care. I believe this so deeply that if I'm preparing for something important, I get nervous if I'm not feeling nervous! I get concerned if I don't have some nervous energy, buzz, or butterflies in my stomach. Why? Because Les was right. If I didn't care, I wouldn't be nervous.

And if I'm not just a little bit nervous, maybe it means I'm not engaged, challenged, or growing. And if I'm not engaged in what I'm doing, then chances are that I'm not growing or enjoying life in a meaningful way. Perhaps I'm wasting my gifts. Cohen's quote whispers to me at times like these, "without continuous personal development, you are now all that you will ever be." It makes the decision to embrace challenges - and those nerves - with eagerness and enthusiasm.

Nowadays, one of my favourite sayings is, "Getting outside your comfort zone is where the magic happens." That's because I understand how pushing yourself outside of your comfort zone puts you into your growth zone. Stretching too far puts you beyond growth and into your panic zone, and that's a place of high stress and anxiety. You have to be bold and humble enough to push yourself into unfamiliar situations and appreciate that the lessons and personal growth are worth the risk.

The most impactful growth comes from doing things that bring us outside of our comfort zone. I believe that strength comes from struggle, so to find magic every day, one of the mantras I've come to embrace is:

> **"WHEN WAS THE LAST TIME YOU DID SOMETHING FOR THE FIRST TIME?"**
>
> - JOHN C. MAXWELL

This quote helps me make decisions when I'm feeling on the spot. Is there an opportunity to learn or connect with people? Then it's worth the potential discomfort. Embracing the pain of new experiences has exponentially accelerated my path. And by accepting my role as a learner, I don't feel silly if I'm not good at something. In fact, I've found that the curiosity in stepping outside my comfort zone has helped endear me to the people around me. The perks here include enhanced connections and even mentorship, which lead to more opportunities to learn and grow.

Many people worry that a leap of faith could result in a belly flop.

Sometimes they feel right and get game-changing results. If you bring an open mind and commitment to learning, the accompanying lesson isn't lost, and the flop isn't repeated.

Research backs up this whole getting outside your comfort zone thing. Psychologists Andy Ryan and Dawn Markova show us three principles of development, or zones, during change: comfort, stretch and stress.

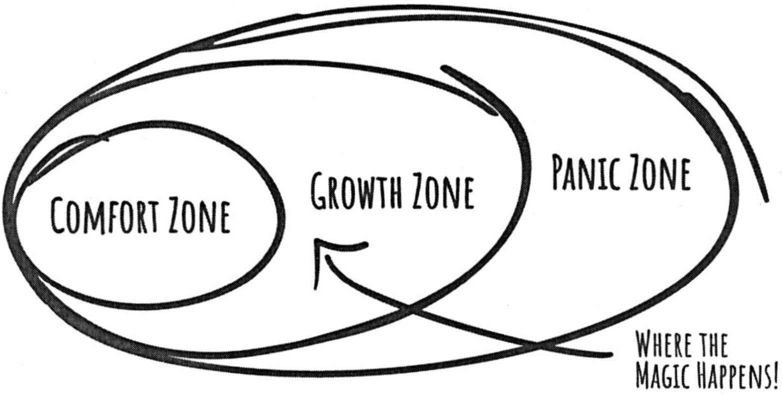

Comfort Zone: Familiar, safe, routine, autopilot, bored. We will find confidence, but the lack of challenge can hinder our ability to find meaning.

Growth/Stretch Zone: Challenge, learning, curiosity. This is where the magic happens!

Panic/Stress Zone: Overwhelmed, exhausted, shut down, stressed. Energy is spent managing anxiety and fears.

In essence, investing in this exercise is a gift of self-awareness; it gives us permission to appreciate the experience of living, and allows us to take the pressure off of ourselves.

If, like me, you believe that "great things never come from comfort zones," then anchoring yourself to your core values will offer you many benefits as you stretch yourself. It starts with understanding your core values - the fundamental beliefs that we have to help us make choices, decisions, and prioritize based on aligning our actions with those beliefs.

Knowing your values will give you:

1. The confidence and courage to try something new;
2. An appreciation of the lessons and the experiences;
3. The ability to adjust your measure of success.

Chapter 1 Exercise

Investing in Alignment - Core Values

In order to answer the first life-changing question, ***What makes me so special?***, we need to start with the basics. We need to understand our values."Values" is another way of saying "the things that I believe are most important to me." They ultimately shape your priorities and will help make decision-making easier.

Alignment is key here - without it, things will never feel quite right, and that makes committing to goals and consistently achieving your dreams impossible. By taking time to reflect on and acknowledge your core values - the ones that remain unwavering over time - you'll be able to align your decisions and actions with those beliefs, and feel more clear and confident in everything you do.

1. Put yourself in the best frame of mind for this exercise by thinking about a recent accomplishment, something you are proud of, and/or a time of happiness and fulfilment. Jot that moment down.
2. Review the list on the next page and select the values that mean the most to you. Add to the list if there is something meaningful to you that's not included here. I want you to think of the ways you are naturally hard-wired to think, feel, and most importantly, do. Start by choosing anything that speaks to you, knowing that you'll ultimately reduce that list down to three to five core values.

Core Values

Abundance
Accountability
Acceptance
Achievement
Adventure
Aesthetic
Ambition
Authenticity
Autonomy
Balance
Belonging
Bravery
Calmness
Cautiousness
Celebration
Clarity
Community
Compassion
Competition
Competency
Confidence
Connection
Consistency
Control
Cooperation
Courage
Creativity
Curiosity
Dependability
Dignity
Diplomacy
Discipline
Discretion
Diversity
Efficiency
Elegance
Empathy
Enthusiasm
Equity
Excellence
Expertise
Fairness
Faith
Family
Fitness
Focus
Freedom
Fresh Thinking
Fun
Grace
Gratitude
Grit
Growth
Happiness
Harmony
Health
Honesty
Honour
Hope
Humour
Humility
Impact
Independence
Influence
Innovation
Insight
Integrity
Joy
Justice
Kindness
Knowledge
Leadership
Learning
Legacy
Loyalty
Love
Mastery
Mindfulness
Originality
Optimism
Passion
Perseverance
Pleasure
Positivity
Preparedness
Prestige
Proactivity
Professionalism
Quality
Recognition
Reliability
Relationships
Reputation
Respect
Responsibility
Resourcefulness
Results
Risk-taking
Safety
Security
Self-Awareness
Self-Control
Serenity
Service
Simplicity
Speed
Spirituality
Stability
Status
Strategy
Strength
Teamwork
Tolerance
Truth
Trust
Uniqueness
Unity
Vision
Value-Add
Vulnerability
Wealth
Wellness
Wisdom

3. If you initially select more than five:
   a. Write each on a sticky note and place them on a large surface.
   b. Try placing the values that mean the most to you at the top.
   c. Reflect on what each of the words means to you and see if any natural cluster words emerge. For example, if you chose "expertise" and "skill/competence" reflect on what each means to you.
   d. Work to eliminate sticky notes by moving them to the bottom of your workspace.

Once you have up to five values (or clusters of values) that you feel good about, jot down a little note about what each means to you.

Here is a sample:

Core Value	How do I want myself or others I serve to say/feel/think?	Cluster Words
Positivity	"That was fun" "That felt good" "I can't wait to do that again"	Fun Passion Pleasure
Community	"I belong here" "I feel included" "I want to contribute my time and energy here"	Belonging Relationships Altruism
Proactivity	"That was easy" "We thought of everything" "We made good use of resources"	Efficiency Credibility
Freedom	"I am able to choose what I do, how I do it, when I do it, and who I do it with"	Creativity Autonomy

Reflection questions:

1. Review your values a day or two after you complete the exercise. How do you feel about the words you chose for your values?
2. Check your answers against some of the big decisions you've made. Were those decisions aligned with your values? Why or why not?

Bonus resources and worksheets are available at: ***www.bestdayeverbook.com/bonus***

"Collect compliments and celebrate 'I've arrived' moments."

- Jessica Potts

2.

Discovering Your Value

How will I make someone's day?

Chapter Purpose:

Have you ever felt useless? It's a helpless, hopeless state where things are happening around you, and you feel as though you aren't able to make a meaningful contribution. It's an awful feeling, especially when you believe in the cause and feel connected to the people.

This chapter's exercise is about understanding the value you bring through the eyes of others, the value that we often take for granted or can't see in ourselves.

This exercise will make you feel validated, motivated, and appreciated. It will also lay the foundation for making informed choices about uncovering your strengths and discovering your passion through service.

I spent the first 30 or so years of my life feeling unclear about my value, my unique contribution. It affected my confidence as I searched for direction and meaning. Most people I've known or worked with across ages, stages, and cultures inherently want:

- To contribute positively to something that we believe in.
- To be valued for our contribution.
- To be of value for the things that light us up and bring us positive energy.

When I say positive energy, I don't mean "vibes." I mean feeling lighter, energized and alive with a kick in your step, not heavier or drained at the end of a task. I mean confidence and enthusiasm. The type that comes from digging into something we are passionate about. I believe that our purpose and passion are best revealed through serving and working with others. Finding ways to put your talents to use and to be appreciated will make you feel good. It will make you want to do more of those things that feel good.

Sounds simple, right?

It was back at the start of my career when the notion of "finding yourself in the service of others" started taking shape in my mind. It happened through the life-changing question:

How will I make someone's day?

In true underdog fashion, my career launch wasn't without its bumps. I had met a guy at school, and we decided to move to his hometown and get hitched. We chose his hometown primarily because his family hosted a weekly Sunday dinner and those family values were important to us (throwback to Chapter 1 - values-based decision-making for the win!).

But graduating with a diploma and a couple of fancy awards didn't equate to a long list of job prospects. We had built relationships in the town where we attended school, and landing interviews for jobs 2.5 hours away, even after attending local job fairs, was proving more challenging than anticipated.

The only job offer I got was from a big box corporate retail company - a retail store that sells, um ... staples. They hired me as a Junior Manager of Retail Service, right at the bottom of the management ladder. Not exactly where the recipient of the first-ever 'Marketing Award for Leadership & Excellence' anticipated landing.

This experience was far outside of my comfort zone. I felt like I had no idea what I was doing. I was the youngest manager in the district with minimal retail or management experience. Worse, I didn't understand or appreciate what made me special or how I could contribute value.

I desperately wished I had been a cashier before becoming a manager. I felt like that would've made me a better manager. My team knew how to do their jobs, but I didn't. I felt helpless, and at times hopeless. I saw solving problems as a big part of my role.

My store was in a state of transition. It was underperforming and in trouble, and the brass was trying to rehabilitate it. That's why they had recently sent an all-star, long-serving general manager from another store to help turn ours around.

I clearly remember leading my first rally meeting - that's the pep talk that kicks off any day in retail. Everyone gathered at the checkouts, the team all wearing their crisp red uniforms. They were mostly veteran team members who had experienced a revolving door of managers, and they were cynical.

The pressure was on. And there it was again.

"IMPOSTER.
IMPOSTER.
IMPOSTER."

I spent some time preparing what I hoped would be a triumphant speech to challenge the team to "go ahead and make someone's day." I wanted to inspire them to be the reason someone else had a great day. I wanted them to do their job so well that our customers left delighted. And if they didn't know how to do that, I encouraged them to just be ... *nice*.

And it worked!

The customers loved it, and my team loved it. They were even reporting back to me about all of the sunshine they were spreading. They were focused on building genuine rapport and serving up solutions. They were so energized from the exercise that the culture change was palpable.

> "THOSE WHO BRING SUNSHINE TO THE LIVES OF OTHERS CAN'T KEEP IT FROM THEMSELVES."
>
> - JAMES M. BARRIE

A focus on serving others was injecting new life into a tired store, and it was changing attitudes. The seed of what would become my best day ever mantra had been sown.

Serendipitously, during the process of writing this book, I stumbled upon my original speech. It was in a portable file folder I maintained early in my career before "the cloud" and online file-sharing was a thing. My original 'dropbox' was a physical box that I've carried with me house-to-house throughout adulthood. I hadn't opened the box in close to 10 years. I found the original speech from 2002 entitled "Go Ahead, Make My Day." Along with a few thank you and farewell notes from past colleagues and clients, I also found employee reviews, a treasure trove of memories, and examples of how I had made an impact.

This box is my original 'Compliment Keeper,' and it has brought me to tears looking through it on more than one occasion. It's even better in hindsight because it affirms the choices I've made and reveals opportunities for how I might add value in new ways today.

Collecting Compliments is the exercise at the end of this chapter. It's an opportunity to reveal more about yourself through others' eyes by seeing patterns as clues. It's particularly useful because we have so much exposure to our own superpowers that it becomes really easy to take our talents for granted. We normalize them instead of honouring and mastering them.

Here's another more recent example of the benefits and usefulness of this exercise. My compliments collection saved me from one of the darkest points in my entrepreneurial career. I was coming off the highest of highs. I had just returned from a business trip to Europe that was my first time leaving the continent. My main squeeze came with me, and we added extra tourist time to the back end of our trip.

After being evicted from the corner office I was renting in a downtown high-rise office building, I had a new home office setup. The eviction sounds more dramatic than it was; the truth is, everyone got kicked out so the new owners could renovate and repurpose the old place. As out-dated as the building was, that corner office, like the Europe trip, represented an "I've arrived" moment. That special milestone in my career was accompanied by a fantastic parking spot marked by a placeholder sign with my logo. Things were going well.

> "THE 'I'VE ARRIVED' MOMENT IS A SPECIAL MILESTONE IN ONE'S CAREER OR LIFE WHERE YOU CAN APPRECIATE THE MOMENT THROUGH THE LENS OF YOUR YOUNGER SELF."
>
> - JESSICA POTTS

I moved my office to my home and things quickly started to get lonely as a solopreneur. Then client projects dried up. Within a couple of short months, I had gone from moving and shaking to lonely and lost. This was all punctuated by personal and family conflicts, where I felt like a victim of unfavourable circumstances. I was in a negative frame of mind and felt positively useless. Remember that helpless-hopeless state of mind I talked about at the start of this chapter? That. I was down in the dumps. I was hanging on to hurt and couldn't be of service to others or myself or see the value I brought to the world — a personal and professional slump.

Weeks went by, and I stumbled upon a scribble in the back of one of my notebooks. It was a short list of compliments that hadn't made it into the compliments file I maintained. In it, I found a few little gems that gave me a glimmer of hope in the dark place I had found myself. The next day I attended a meeting for a volunteer community organization. It was so nice to get out of the house and connect with the people around the table that included someone I've admired and looked up to for a couple of years, Darien. He always had a genuine interest in my career and community endeavours. He offered great advice whenever I sought his input.

One of my scribble compliments is from him. I wanted to let him know how much it lifted my spirits in that dark time, so I asked him for coffee to catch up, as we would typically do a couple of times a year for the few years we'd known each other. A week later, Darien and I met for coffee, and easy chatting ensued. After a few minutes, he looked at me sincerely and said, "So kid, what did you want to talk about?"

I gave him the quick but punctuated version of my current slump, sparing him the details to get to the punch line. I let him know I had stumbled upon his compliment and how much it meant that he had seen something great in me. I surprised myself by getting emotional and needed to fight back the tears explaining the compliment he hadn't even remembered giving. Here's how the conversation went:

"Remember when you were in the running for that big job last year?" I asked. "Yes, of course," he replied.

I continued, "Well, you had asked me if I had a day or two a week available from my consulting business to work on a project with you. You saw me being the perfect person to meet with stakeholders and find out what their issues were because my approachable nature encourages people to open up, while my strategic nature helps to probe deeper and connect themes to broader goals and solutions."

"I do remember that now," he said.

"I just needed to say thank you. Finding that compliment reminded me of how I can use my talents to serve others. You reminded me how my unique contribution could add value, and that helped me see myself differently in my darkest moments," I replied.

He was touched that he had made such a meaningful impact. Then the wheels in his brain started turning. He pondered and paused before he spoke.

"Hmmm ... that's interesting ... I have another project that could use that skill set."

We talked about an exciting opportunity that met my criteria of working on "cool projects with cool people" and tapped into the talents I love leveraging. Two weeks later, with clarity about my value, my confidence restored, and the courage I needed to seek new opportunities, I landed five gigs in one week. One a day that week. It was a year's worth of contracts and included the single biggest gig of my entrepreneurial career.

Now all of that didn't happen because of one compliment, but it represented a significant turning point I don't take for granted.

Chapter 2 Exercise

Collecting Compliments

Collecting Compliments is an exercise that you'll complete over time, with impactful results. Start now by creating a Compliment Keeper and adding to it as you receive positive feedback in any area of your life.

You'll need:

- Your own Compliment Keeper (a recipe box and blank index cards, or a binder and page protectors for notes/cards).

Steps:

1. Think of the nicest compliment(s) you've received.
2. Use one index card per compliment. Include enough detail to jog the memory of your future self. Note things like:
    a. Who complimented you;
    b. The date or time period;
    c. The context - who that person is to you, and perhaps why their feedback is important/relevant;
    d. The compliment.
3. Keep adding to your Compliment Keeper as you receive nice feedback, kudos, and recognition for the impact you've made in people's lives. Print emails and screenshots from your social media accounts as people say nice things. Keep thank-you notes.

4. Schedule time in your calendar to review it and look for ways to repeat the behaviour that earned you the compliment.
5. When you are feeling down or glum, make time to go through your compliments. Reach out and thank one person who has made an impact on you through their feedback.

Note: Feedback is a gift. Honest, sincere feedback is tough to find. You can also collect constructive feedback, as long as you can validate their influence.

Reflection questions:

1. Jot down words and phrases that people have used to describe you.
2. Looking back at previous compliments, do you notice any patterns?
3. How can you repeat the behaviour that earned you the compliment?
4. Among what scenarios and people do you seem to thrive?

Bonus resources and worksheets are available at: ***www.bestdayeverbook.com/bonus***

"Stretching yourself with sincerity and curiosity is key to growing into the person you are destined to be."

- Jessica Potts

3.

Authentically You

What's Keeping Me From Being My Most Authentic Self?

Chapter Purpose:

Have you ever had an authenticity crisis? Maybe you felt unsure about who you are and the value you provide? Perhaps you felt like you were doing things more to please others than to be true to yourself? Or maybe you're already feeling clear and need some strategies to move forward?

This chapter's exercise is about communicating your value and values to the world to attract the right people, opportunities, and experiences. Who are you? What lights you up? How can you help? Whether establishing yourself, pivoting your career, or evolving your offering, being clear on your personal brand will help you plant your flag and shout from the rooftops.

Building a solid reputation for your expertise and establishing credibility in your chosen field is one of the most important things you can do in your working life. When you communicate who you are with consistency, you build your personal brand and set yourself up for success - and in this case, 'success' equals doing more of what you love.

What do you want to be known for? Where is the gap? How do you gain the credibility and confidence to deliver on your promise?

My retail career was short-lived. I generally liked my job and the people I worked with. Still, I realized that the lifestyle that accompanied retail hours wasn't going to suit me in the long term. The nail in the coffin on that part of my career was when I could not commit to a weekend canoe trip for my mom's 50th birthday. It was still more than three months away, but my store was short on managers who could open and close, so I couldn't commit.

This made me realize that a career in retail wasn't going to align with the lifestyle I desired or the values I held. So, when someone sent me a job posting that they thought I was well-suited for, I jumped at it. The role involved operating a government resource centre for entrepreneurs, which sounded great. It was based out of a local City Hall building, which seemed like a step up from my unpredictable retail role. The only catch - the salary was about 10% less than my current job was, even before the retail bonus.

Fun fact: every career move I've made was for the same or less money, but had intangible lifestyle benefits that I placed a monetary value on.

That was a pretty big pay gap for someone just starting out, but I valued the freedom of having weekends off to spend time with those I loved, so I went for it. I felt proud of myself during the interviews - like I had put my best foot forward, as my grandmother would say.

When I was hired, I was the youngest person working in City Hall at the tender age of 23. My mom and gram took me shopping at a high-quality second-hand shop where I could find blouses and blazers that would help me feel more confident. I took hand-me-downs from family members too. Coming from a uniformed retail environment where the biggest fashion decisions were long-sleeved or short-sleeved, my new City Hall wardrobe was an important part of feeling accepted in the job.

Nevertheless, I spent the first six months feeling like I didn't have much value to contribute to my clients and my role. I still remember the day I realized that crying at my desk instead of the washroom would save time (half-joking). Though I had other skills that fit the position, I ran a resource centre for launching and growing businesses, and I barely knew the first thing about starting a business. The imposter thing was real. I mean, I was advising people on how to start and grow their businesses. And I had never run my own business! The little voice was back heckling again.

**"IMPOSTER.
IMPOSTER.
IMPOSTER."**

Adding to my inferiority complex and imposter syndrome was one of my new co-workers. Tanya and I started the same day in different departments. She was also young, only a year or two older than me, but didn't seem to have the same confidence issues that I did. At all. While I was in my stuffy navy blue slacks and jackets, she was in jeans and one-shoulder shirts going down maintenance holes! We can argue the practicality of that later - the point here is that she oozed confidence.

She had found a niche early in her career. She worked in the engineering department and seemed to not only have important work but also seemed to fit in with her peers seamlessly. She belonged. She was funny, confident, and outspoken. Truly one of the most authentic people I knew. I was in awe of her in so many ways - most of all, she was unapologetic about who she was. And that made her absolutely magnetic.

Her bold authenticity became abundantly clear the day she asked me (a version of) my next life-changing question:

"Why do you dress like a librarian?"

Now, let me be clear; she wasn't wrong when she dropped this truth bomb on me. And she wasn't trying to hurt or insult me with the question. The way she said it was kinda like, "you're too cool to dress like a stereotypical version of a 1980s librarian." In those hand-me-down clothes, I absolutely looked like someone else that wasn't me.

What she was really saying was that I wasn't *authentic*.

The candour that accompanied her life-changing question was the basis of what became a deep and enduring friendship. In fact, I served as one of her bridesmaids and wedding emcees, and over a decade later, she still sends me up-to-date headshots when I refresh the slides for my keynote speeches! So the real life-changing question-behind-the-question was:

What's keeping me from being my most authentic self?

Her question forced me to examine why I felt that I HAD to dress like a librarian and the answer surprised me: I was being the person I *thought* my clients wanted me to be. I wasn't comfortable with my value or aware enough of who I was to just be myself. I was too busy being who I thought others wanted me to be. So I spent a lot of time figuring out who I really was and the contribution I made. Two of the most important lessons at the time were:

1. Being afraid to show your authentic self directly impacts your ability to build trust and meaningful connections. It begs the question: "What else is she hiding?"
2. I don't have to hide my quirks to provide value to my clients and have them take me seriously.

I found that working on my personal brand - a relatively new concept at the time - could help me define and communicate my value and boost my confidence by understanding how my skills, knowledge, and personality make me relevant to my clients, colleagues, and beyond.

Great personal brands are:

- Uncovered, not manufactured. It's already inside of you.
- Rooted in the value you provide to your intended audience. This is the part that keeps you relevant.
- Easy to remember and repeat. Make it easy for people to refer others to you. It's about being recognized for your talents and facilitating that.
- All about consistency.

"REPUTATIONS THRIVE ON REPETITION."

- WILLIAM ARRUDA

An important piece of this is the aspirational side. To whom and how do you want to be of service? What currently separates you from that goal?

In my conversations and classrooms, the adage "fake it til you make it" gets mixed reviews because it's not authentic. It's not about pretending to be something you're not.

Stretching yourself with sincerity and curiosity is the key to growing into the person you are destined to be with courage and confidence.

Here's a simple example: a close friend recently shared a video on her social media channels, speaking perfect French. I was blown away! I didn't know she could speak French at all, let alone fluently.

When I complimented her on it, she replied that it felt awkward, like she was exaggerating or faking it, but she leaned into it anyway, and it came off really well.

This notion of stretching yourself ties back to one of the anchoring concepts of this system and book. Getting outside your comfort zone is key to doing something that you aren't quite ready to do. Tackling the challenge ignites you, and magic ensues.

If we study hard enough to mimic a master, isn't that the path to mastery?

Chapter 3 Exercise

Personal Branding Statement

An exercise like this needs to be centered around your audience and their needs while showcasing your uniqueness and the challenges you crave.

This is an introductory exercise that will help you define yourself and create a personal branding statement (think: Linkedin headline, or Instagram biography), or even outline key points to craft your biography. This is not an advanced exercise on how to create a personal brand strategy to produce relevant content. It took me quite some time to find a way to define and label my personal brand statement to reflect the right combination of:

- audience-centric and relevant
- authentic and unique
- reflecting my passion

I had built my identity around providing value for entrepreneurs and aspiring business owners. But I needed something that transcended the context of the paid job I had. My first personal brand statement – *Facilitating your awesomeness and inspiring your Best Day Ever* – was created when I was in my late 20s through this process.

A common format is:

I help (*describe your audience/who you serve*) **to** (*describe the outcome/result*).

You may have more than one reply depending on who is asking and how you may provide value to them. My most recent iteration of this statement for my leadership and team development training programs is:

I help leaders build their dream teams.

You want your answer to evoke the response, "How do you do that?" which allows you to share a relatable story or anecdote that highlights your passion and purpose in a short case study. Your answer should showcase your capabilities and make it easy for people to understand your expertise and what they could call on you for. People naturally want to help and deepen a connection.

Reflection questions:

1. How can you incorporate your values from exercise one?
2. How can you incorporate the feedback and compliments from exercise two?
3. How can you show your uniqueness compared to others in your field?
4. How can you embrace your *road wear* to be more unique and relatable? (reference Chapter 6)

Bonus resources and worksheets are available at: **www.bestdayeverbook.com/bonus**

"Positive energy is a powerful thing. It attracts opportunity like a magnet."

- Jessica Potts

4.

Discovering Your Passion

How will I discover my passion?

Chapter Purpose:

It's easy to feel lost and discouraged in life, especially when you are unclear about your purpose. It becomes hard to find meaning, which feels like wandering aimlessly.

This type of discouragement isn't something that happens exclusively in one's formative years. Like the global pandemic that turned our world upside down, you likely found yourself in a different mindset, role, or circumstance. It probably made you question your purpose or relevance. I know I have, at numerous points in my life.

This chapter's exercise is about gaining clarity in order to understand what makes you so special! These are the clues that will lead you to discover your passion and gain the confidence and courage to pursue your purpose.

My authenticity crisis from Chapter 3 continued on a day that started like any ordinary day. I didn't know it when I woke up, but this was a day that would change the course of my life forever, and it all started in a Grade 10 careers class - not as a student, but as a guest presenter in my early 20s.

Part of my role at the business resource centre was to promote youth entrepreneurship enthusiastically. Keep in mind this was right on the cusp of entrepreneurship being considered cool by the mainstream. My office administered a summer funding program that would help students start and run their businesses to promote entrepreneurship as a career option for a younger generation.

So there I am in front of a classroom full of students, pumping up small business and entrepreneurship, when a girl who couldn't have been more than 14 years old asked a question that hit me like a punch in the face. It would become one of the most punctuating, life-changing questions in all of my years to date and since. She said, "If you think small business is so great, why don't you have one?"

"IMPOSTER.
IMPOSTER.
IMPOSTER."

This time, my little inner voice added "HYPOCRITE" to the chant. I did think small business was great. I did believe in entrepreneurship and the amazing clients I had been serving.

Yet, I had never even considered starting my own business. I mean, what would or could I even do? What was I so intensely passionate about that I could create a business and mould my life around? I was in my mid-twenties and still figuring out what I wanted to be when I grew up.

Like many at the time, I'd never thought entrepreneurship was an option. Growing up, I didn't know anyone who was an entrepreneur. As a young adult, I loved my steady paycheque and the stability and security of a regular job. The spotlight and supports for entrepreneurs didn't exist then in the same way they do today. This was all happening during the infancy of e-commerce and social media, which changed everything, especially for the younger, more tech-savvy generation.

Those 13 words had as much impact as any other words I'd ever heard. If you think small business is so great, why don't you have one? They echoed through my head and started renting space in my brain. So while I don't remember exactly how I answered that question at the moment, I do remember how I answered it over time. (Spoiler alert: I ended up starting a small business.)

Once again, I was forced to face that all-important question: "What makes me so special?" This time, it was through the lens of passion. I still didn't understand what made me special, and I couldn't figure out what I was passionate about. Wasn't it supposed to be easy? Just "follow your passion," as my high school guidance counsellor and many others had said.

Entrepreneurs surrounded me. They were - and are - the single most passionate group of people I had ever known, pursuing their dreams and making things happen. That led me to start thinking to myself. How will I follow my passion?

I started studying what passion meant. I thought that if I could follow my passion, then maybe I'd find the fast-track to success and happiness. Passion was the hack or the shortcut, I thought. So while I want to tell you to go out and triumphantly follow your passion, what I found was both fascinating and frustrating.

It turns out you have to do your time. There's no magic passion fairy ready to sprinkle the seeds of success onto you while you sleep. There's no conveyor belt of passions that lets you choose one or two that look juicy. "I'll take one of those ... and two of those". That's just not how it works. And part of my frustration is that I grew up hearing those three words: "Follow Your Passion."

Many of us have heard this before. We came up in an age where the phrase was a cultural phenomenon. Then I found an article in the *Harvard Business Review* by Cal Newport that summarized exactly how I was feeling. Newport explained that the term "follow" implies that you *start* with a passion and *match* it to an existing job. It implies that you should love your work from the very first day!

The article included a Google tool that shows the occurrences of the phrase "Follow Your Passion" in printed English over time. It starts in 1980 – the year I was born – and it rose sharply during the formative years of career development for 1980's kids. Around 2000, the use of the phrase "Follow Your Passion" just took off!

So, getting back to that life-changing question: "How will I follow my passion?" We need to take control of our stories and give ourselves space and time to answer the real question that Newport highlighted:

How will I discover my passion?

We need to change the narrative and talk about the struggles of finding your place. Newport says "If you study people who LOVE what they do for a living, you'll find that in most cases their passion developed slowly, often over unexpected and complicated paths."

> "NOT ALL THOSE WHO WANDER ARE LOST."
>
> - J.R.R. TOLKIEN

Today's workforce will pivot in their careers more than any generation before. The path is not straight. It's up to us to take control and ownership of our own paths. We need to understand that failure is an option. In fact, being curious, getting outside your comfort zone, and being open to failure by trying new things is the most effective way to discover your passion.

We need to embrace our struggles and learn to trust them. In many cases, you'll discover things that you don't like or don't feel good about. Those are important clues to your passion, too (reference Chapter 8).

Positive energy is a powerful thing. It attracts opportunity like a magnet, and it makes you feel alive. It's also a sign that you're on the right path - that you are tapping into your natural sources of talent and potential. And guess what? That powerful, compelling feeling that often accompanies positive energy is PASSION!

Chapter 4 Exercise

Proud, Productive and Providing Value

Think of a time when you felt productive, successful, and of value. Think of a time when you felt positive and confident. It doesn't have to be grand – it could be a simple activity where you just felt like you were firing on all cylinders. Maybe it was a task around the house, an interaction at work or school, or working towards a fitness goal. Perhaps it was a small moment in your day, a part of your routine or a bigger project.

What aspects of this experience made you feel alive, accomplished, or proud? If you're stuck, read my example below.

Cooking dinner for my family is an everyday example of feeling productive, successful, and valuable. Simple, right? It may not seem like much, but it's impressive with a bit more context.

First, I'm probably in the top percentile of pickiest eaters on the planet. I'm working on it - now, for example, I eat salad with dressing - and a host of other "grown-up" enhancements.

Second, in what my mother calls a "cosmic feat of karmic retribution," one of my kids inherited the picky gene from me. And at the tender age of eight, he claimed vegetarian status – though his definition in practice is light on actual vegetables.

Finally, I'm not a particularly good cook, nor am I creative with healthy ideas. Nor do I maintain a Pinterest board or recipe book that will suit the diverse palates at my table – so the struggle is real when it comes to dinner prep.

Luckily for me, it's not the act of cooking or mastering the flavour fusion, or even the artistic presentation that gives me a deep sense of satisfaction. It's the challenge of managing and synchronizing the different aspects of dinner into a triumphant culminating moment that I find fulfilling. Having each component of the meal prepped, plated, and on the table at the right time brings me joy. That's the critical factor that keeps me challenged and engaged.

When I reflected on it, I realized that this example also explains many of my most fulfilling career accomplishments, plenty of which centre around organizing events with multiple moving parts that culminate in a memorable or transformative experience for participants.

Now back to your own example of a time you felt productive, successful, and valuable. Think of how good that felt. The quiet satisfaction you felt as you took a deep breath, admired your effort, and appreciated the result.

Pay close attention to those times – they'll reveal your deep motivations and your greatest potential for replicating that feeling of productivity, success, and providing value. In positive psychology some call it a flow state. Others close to me call it being "in your element" – it's inspiring, insightful and downright energizing. It lights you up, and you feel like you can conquer anything. That's your passion at play!

"PAY ATTENTION TO THE THINGS YOU ARE NATURALLY DRAWN TO. THEY ARE OFTEN CONNECTED TO YOUR PATH, PASSION, AND PURPOSE IN LIFE. HAVE THE COURAGE TO FOLLOW THEM."

- RUBEN CHAVEZ

Now imagine you could bottle it. Imagine you could feel that satisfaction every day. Putting your unique talents to use consistently and intentionally is the key to channelling that power into positive energy. In the darkest times, leaning into the things that bring out your passion and doing more of the things we are naturally hard-wired to do is the key to living your best day ever every day!

Reflection question:

1. Think of a time when you felt productive, successful, and valuable. What aspects of this experience made you feel alive, accomplished, or proud?

Bonus resources and worksheets are available at: ***www.bestdayeverbook.com/bonus***

"Personality quirks hold powerful clues."

– Jessica Potts

5.

Everyone Has Talent

How will I play to my strengths?

Chapter Purpose:

We live in a culture fixated on flaws and fixing weaknesses. It's created a world of pressure, stress, illness, and exhaustion. Too often, we measure ourselves by comparison instead of understanding, harnessing, and leveraging our uniqueness toward our goals. A lack of self-worth can be devastating.

This chapter's exercise is about replacing the question "What makes me so special?" with a different question that breeds hope over cynicism and empowerment over comparison:

"How can I play to my strengths?"

This exercise is about focusing on what's right with you, not fixating on what's wrong. It will help you find clarity, confidence, direction, and success by nurturing your natural strengths.

Things started changing for me in my later 20s - for the better. I was asked to join a new networking group for young people that I qualified for at the time. This was another one of my "I've arrived" moments.

It was one of those exclusive one-per-industry networking groups, and members were some of the most decorated up-and-comers in my area. I was honoured to be included amongst these over-achievers. But I was also humbled and very self-conscious because I didn't quite feel I had earned my seat at the cool kids' table. What had I done that was so important? What made me so special? The little inner heckler was back with a vengeance!

"IMPOSTER.
IMPOSTER.
IMPOSTER."

About six months after joining the group, I found myself in my friend's office - the same friend who invited me to the group in the first place.

He asks me, "So ... what do you think of the group?"

"I love it!" I answered honestly, but not completely.

He wasn't convinced. "Buuuuuuut?"

"Well, if I'm totally honest, it's really humbling. You guys are all at the top of your game." I paused, contemplating my vulnerability in saying it out loud. "And it leaves me wondering, what makes me so special?"

BOOM. There it was. My vulnerability laid out atop his desk. At the time, being vulnerable wasn't my thing.

Hearing those words, he sat up abruptly, pushed his chair back, reached into a box on his filing cabinet, and handed me the book that would change my life, but I didn't know that yet. In fact, I was super skeptical, which sounded something like:

"Oh, what's this?" I asked.

"It's a self-help book!" he replied.

Dripping with sarcasm, but trying to politely disguise it as enthusiasm, I muttered, "Ohhh ... great ... another self-help book!"

He responded, "No, no, this one is different. It has an ASSESSMENT!"

With a little more sarcasm than enthusiasm, this time, I replied, "Ohhh ... great ... another assessment!""

I had had enough of assessments. Between schooling, my modest career experience to date, and my recent passion exercise, I felt like I had done them all. At that point, I didn't see a lot of value in personality assessments. So, as you might expect, I took that book, tucked it away (in this case, in the backseat of my little red pick up truck), and promptly forgot all about it.

Lucky for me, my friend was in sales, so persistence was a talent of his. He followed up with me about the book and the assessment, and after a couple of weeks, I finally did it. But this assessment wasn't like the others. It gave me a magic moment of realization! An epiphany. An "aha moment".

The book that changed my life is called "StrengthsFinder 2.0." Rooted in over 50 years of Gallup research, it is based on Dr. Donald O. Clifton's question: "What would happen if we studied what's right with people versus what's wrong with them?"

Here are my three biggest takeaways:

1. What makes you so special is already inside you. Everyone has talent. It shows up in our natural ways of thinking, feeling, and behaving. Talents, when applied consistently and productively towards a goal, result in strength.
2. It can be easy to take your unique talents for granted, mistaking them for personality quirks instead of powerful clues that reveal your purpose and unlock your potential.
3. On the flip side, too much of a good thing (your natural talents/tendencies) can lead to unintended (negative) results. Your weaknesses are often misapplications of your talent, rather than a lack of it.

This assessment made a lot of sense to me, and not in the

horoscopy way that some assessments do, and it perfectly articulated what made me so special!

As I read the report about my unique talents and how to positively apply them as strengths, a growth cycle started in me that I've since witnessed with the hundreds of friends and clients I have worked with since graduating from the first Canadian cohort of Gallup Certified Strengths Coaches.

Strengths-based development is about becoming more of who you already are and applying it to your unique circumstances or context. It's about managing your natural tendencies productively to feel more energized and engaged in all aspects of your life. It pinpointed and explained the parts of my personality that had most contributed to my success and gave me a guide to using those talents consistently and effectively.

So the key to feeling energized, fulfilled, and productive is in harnessing the power of your unique talents. It starts with knowing yourself - your hot buttons, triggers, motivators, reflecting on how you can provide value, and taking meaningful action.

It helped me accept who I am and see how I can share my gifts. It helped me apply my talent to grow as a person. It helped to inspire meaningful action that gets results. It gave me *hope.*

Here is an impactful personal example of these concepts tied together in a realization that is both embarrassing and inspiring.

The CliftonStrengths Assessment identified one of my top talents as being WOO, which stands for "Winning Others Over." The hallmarks of this talent include enjoying the challenge of breaking the ice and making connections with new people.

I recognized it in myself immediately but didn't want to admit or acknowledge it. Growing up, I was quite social and even modestly popular, but not in a traditional way. I could make friends easily through my charm but sometimes wore out my welcome quickly with my intensity and high energy. In other words, I was annoying. It was the same natural instinct (e.g. talent) that was driving both outcomes - charming and annoying. The problem was I couldn't recognize it or apply that talent intentionally and with discipline, so I was like a wild horse trying to finish the Kentucky Derby.

As I learned in StrengthsFinder 2.0, too much of a good thing can have unintended consequences. By maturing and developing my talents, I've learned to dial it down (a bit) or put myself into situations where that natural talent is an asset, like finding the balance between remaining authentic and effervescent versus intense and annoying.

Maybe you can relate to that story, whether it's the same charming vs. annoying example or similar patterns of behaviour.

Here are three more examples from the workplace:

1. Maybe you're a natural "numbers person" with a flair for

finding trends and patterns. Be careful that your love of analysis doesn't keep you from taking action while there's still time.

2. Maybe you're a natural "people person" and you find it easy to develop relationships. Be careful that your love of building connections doesn't cause you to make deals at the expense of profit.
3. Maybe you're an "ideas person" and skilled at coming up with brilliant concepts. Be careful that your love of the creative process doesn't stop you from producing a tangible result.

These examples of talents misapplied would be considered weaknesses in Gallup's definition of strengths-based development. So it's not about trying to compensate for who you aren't; it's about harnessing and managing who you already *are*.

The timing for this assessment was great because things at the office and in my life were at a low, and I was in a rut. My best friend at work had moved on, I had a disengaged leader, dealt with a workplace bully, marriage troubles had started brewing, and I was generally feeling down. Looking back, it was one of the lowest points of my working life.

Adding to the frustration was a bad case of colleague envy. I was envious of how engaged a colleague was. He was in the same role as me, but he was better at it. He seemed to just know what to do, and he was even passionate about it. It was infuriating and certainly didn't help with the imposter syndrome. I needed something I could be passionate about, and I could feel the opportunity to not only "discover my passion," but also to answer the next life-changing question:

How will I play to my strengths?

I dove in head first and put the results of my strengths-based development exercise into action. I would use my talents to rally myself, my clients, and the community around a signature annual event celebrating small business. The downtown was undergoing a revitalization. I hatched a plan to utilize new spaces on the main strip for workshops and seminars to showcase the evolving downtown and generate some buzz. Guided by my strengths assessment and the ideas for action, I put together a plan to leverage my talents and started reaching out to my contacts.

First was the publisher of the local newspaper. This was just before social media became mainstream. I pitched my idea about showcasing the artist spaces to him, and he loved it! Before the end of our call, he had pledged five figures of advertising to boost the event. I was so excited and felt so validated. I hung up the phone and ran over to my colleague in the next office. I told her what had happened and proudly proclaimed that *"Today is the best day ever!"*

And so it began.

The next day was very much the same, more energizing calls to my contacts and other stakeholders. Everyone was supporting the event. That day I also hung up the phone and proclaimed

"Today is the best day ever!"

It went on.

In speaking to people I was hearing feedback that my passion and enthusiasm was contagious - exactly what my strengths report had said! And the event was a hit — a huge, resounding success. And so my best day ever, strengths-based experiment was proven!

I was on fire. I felt energized and alive, and I wanted to work harder because of it. That's the magical thing about strengths-based development. It makes you feel *awesome*. With this lens of strengths-based development, I could grow by focusing on what's right with me, not fixating on what's wrong with me.

- Things became clear that had once been foggy.
- Doubt and skepticism faded, and confidence emerged.
- Where I once felt lost, I now felt I had direction.

"IMPOSTER.
IMPOSTER.
IMPOSTER."

The little heckler that shouted these words now had to work a whole lot harder. I could finally articulate my value. Even better, I had an action plan for success.

This gave me a way to validate and replicate my successes. The cycle of Strengths-based Development I experienced, which would evolve into the system that inspired this book (Clarity, Confidence, Courage) was:

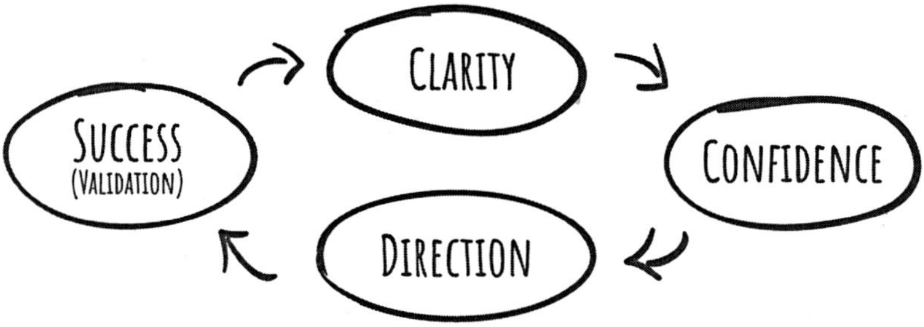

Chapter 5 Exercise

Unlock Your Talent

Complete a personality assessment. There are many out there, but Gallup's CliftonStrengths Assessment is hands down my favourite.

Note: I receive no compensation for recommending that assessment - Gallup doesn't have an affiliate program or offer kickbacks of any kind. As you read in the chapter, I've done many assessments but no other provided the same eye-opening, action-oriented impact that this one has.

Reflection Questions:

Once you've completed the assessment and reviewed your report, look back to your example(s) from the Chapter 4 exercise.

1. What insights and themes are you able to connect between your report and your example in Chapter 4?
2. What insights does your report reveal about how you can have more consistent, positive outcomes by managing your talent productively (like my charming vs annoying example)?
3. What is one thing you will commit to doing differently? How will you know you're successful?

Bonus resources and worksheets are available at: ***www.bestdayeverbook.com/bonus***

"The seeds
of your success
are sown through
your struggles."

- Jessica Potts

6.

Calculated Risks

What would I do if I had nothing to lose?

Chapter Purpose:

As the old saying goes - one thing that's constant is change. And I've found this often happens when we're just getting settled into a routine or a way of life. That can make us feel a range of emotions from slightly unbalanced or helpless to full-blown victim mentality.

The best way I've found to be poised for whatever life brings is to evaluate risks holistically when making decisions. I do this by considering my values, strengths, and how I can serve myself and those I lead.

This exercise is a simple reflection that may shift your perspective and turn road wear into the foundation for a best day ever.

When we left off in Chapter 5, things were starting to look up for me. I had just discovered Strengths-based Development and gained the clarity, confidence, and courage to validate and replicate my success.

That amazing process led to my *best day ever* happening several days in a row.

I wouldn't get to ride that wave for long because life was about to take a big turn. I was about to trade in my pickup truck for a minivan. Why? I found out I was pregnant - surprise! I had just applied for a new job, and I felt very torn. Should I still be pursuing the new job? I knew what my legal rights were; it wasn't that. It was that I would only have a few months on the job before my new prospective employer would have to find my replacement.

I wondered if I could make the impact I wanted to in the new office in that short time? Would I miss sharing all of my pregnancy milestones with "The Lunch Bunch," an eclectic crew of ladies from different departments who ate together and supported each other regularly?

There were consequences of not leaving too — risks to my personal and professional growth. I had been in an entry-level position for six years. The role had evolved to include supervisory responsibilities, special projects, and a fair amount more money than when I started. But the job title remained the same, and the opportunities for promotion were limited.

Shortly after finding out I was pregnant, I had a scare that sent me to the hospital. I left in good health but didn't know if the 5-week embryo inside me still had a heartbeat. I realized at that moment how much I loved this baby already and wanted better for both of us.

But I still wasn't convinced about applying for the new job until I met with two mentors over the holidays. Both couldn't believe that I was considering withdrawing my application because of the pregnancy. And both felt strongly about what I should do. They both highlighted the risk of *not* pursuing the role. What if I stepped away from the competition and lost the baby? It would be doubly devastating.

So I did, and I got the job. But now I had an even bigger chip on my shoulder - I felt that I had to prove (to myself) that I was worthy of the new role. I put in three weeks of overtime in the last six months of my pregnancy. I identified so strongly with my career role that I had many insecurities in stepping away to become a mom. My self-worth was utterly tied to my job performance. What if my replacement was better than me at the job?

Adding to that, motherhood was way tougher than I anticipated. I wasn't a bad mom to my baby, but I wasn't good at it either. I didn't know a hungry cry from a sleepy cry. I loved my child but couldn't wait to get back to work. I returned from maternity leave #1 and hit the ground running. Two months later, I was emceeing a high-profile event and feeling like I was at the top of my game again. Grateful to be back doing something I felt good at.

A week later, I found out I was pregnant again. Surprise! I'm not trying to gloss over the next year or so, but sleep deprivation with two kids under two years old is *real*, and it's all a blur. What I can tell you is that my world was flipped upside down, and everything changed once my kids arrived.

I had a lot of trouble accepting my new role and my new life.

As with my first maternity leave, I was slated to return early. A few weeks before my official return-to-work date, I visited the office on April Fools' Day. My new boss was there and I took the opportunity to have an informal chat with him about my return to work. We talked about the nitty-gritty stuff like getting email access. Then I broached the subject of flexible working hours to promote the office's services to the entrepreneurs we served. Entrepreneurs aren't 9-to-5 people, so in order to stay relevant and connected, I knew I'd have to attend evening meetings and events to reach them. As a new mom, I didn't think I should have to give up time with my kids to do that.

I used the example of an evening event happening on my first scheduled day back at work and asked if I could come in late the next day. The response was a wince, followed by a dialogue about why it wouldn't work, and ending with an offer for me to put together a formal proposal about what the arrangement could look like.

It wasn't the work of putting together a proposal that turned me off. It was the complete misalignment with my values. It was the rampant bureaucracy that stifles creativity and general awesomeness. I hadn't heard this quote at the time, but I could certainly appreciate it when I read it years later:

> "THE OBLIGATION FOR WORKING MOTHERS IS A VERY PRECISE ONE: THE FEELING THAT ONE OUGHT TO WORK AS IF ONE DID NOT HAVE CHILDREN, WHILE RAISING ONE'S CHILDREN AS IF ONE DID NOT HAVE A JOB."
>
> - ANNABEL CRABB

I was at a crossroads.

One week later I was speaking with a colleague from a partnering organization with whom I had kept in close contact over my maternity leave. Jeff was pumped up, having just received extra funding for his office. But there was a problem - he needed a senior-level marketing, communications, and community engagement team member but only had the budget for a junior role.

We hung up the phone, and my mind started racing. My expertise was in marketing, communications, and community engagement. We both had a problem, and we both seemed to have an answer to the other's problem - he just didn't know it yet. The words of the high school student who challenged me during my presentation almost 10 years earlier echoed again through my head:

"If you think small business is so great, why don't you have one?"

Until that point I didn't know what I could do that would satisfy my passion, leverage my strengths, provide a challenge, AND have the opportunity to support myself and my family. I knew it would work financially because we were already living very humbly while my then-husband was back at school. We knew how to stretch a budget. With this perspective and a large 'anchor client' guaranteeing me steady work with flexibility, I could have the freedom to pursue other clients and opportunities with stability and security.

My life had changed drastically. To balance my new priorities, I knew something had to change. It all just made so much sense. So with budgeting out of the way, the question became:

What will I do when I have nothing to lose?

That's a daring statement because leaving a great job with salary, benefits, and a pension could definitely count as having something to lose. In fact, many people would soon tell me that I was downright crazy for leaving my 'cushy' government job.

Was there risk in starting a business? Absolutely.

The consequences of not taking a chance, a calculated risk, or a leap of faith can be severe. I think of an example of someone I used to know, let's call her Agnes. She also worked in government, starting as an intern, and staying on with the department. She disliked her role, coworkers, and general working arrangement. She seemed to dislike just about everything, always finding ways to complain about her circumstances. She was never satisfied with any aspect of her life.

Some people in life serve as a role model of how NOT to behave. Agnes was that for me.

She was becoming my definition of pessimism, unhappiness, and victim mentality. One day I asked her what she would rather be doing with her life. She said that she always wanted to be a stay-at-home mom, but she and her husband couldn't afford it.

At the same time, she and her husband could afford two brand new vehicles, destination vacations, and an extravagant renovation to their home. Agnes failed to see how those lifestyle decisions were not aligned with her values and priorities. Her misery would continue to fester.

There was definitely risk in quitting my job and starting a business. But I also appreciated Agnes as a living, breathing example of the risks of not taking action. With that, I had a sense of confidence and assuredness that I had never experienced before. It was almost like a high. And it wasn't that I thought my business would be wildly successful. It was a deep understanding of the consequences of not recalibrating my lifestyle to align with my values and priorities.

For once, I felt clear and confident in my decision.
For once, I didn't feel like an imposter.
For once, I was in full alignment.

I called my friend, colleague, and prospective first client back 10 minutes later. I told him that he could hire me - I would quit my job and start my own business to allow me the flexibility I needed while staying a part of the network I loved. In return, he would get someone qualified and ready to hit the ground running, with intimate knowledge of the programs, partners, and clients. It was perfect.

And he said yes! I had my first client. Now I just needed a business! Two weeks later – on the day I had initially planned on returning to work - I instead registered and launched my own business and became an accidental entrepreneur. I'd go on to make a lot of mistakes in business. I'd win projects and clients, and I'd lose projects and clients. I'd always take time to reflect on the lessons learned to help accelerate whatever lay ahead. I'd also appreciate the modest success of replacing my government income with the added flexibility of self-employment.

Nelson Mandela said, "I never lose. Either I win or I learn." What if we adopted an attitude where we never lose? Where failure isn't the opposite of success, it's part of success. In the entrepreneurial world, particularly in Silicon Valley, where life would soon take me, there is a mantra, "fail fast and move on."

I'm not suggesting that starting a business will ease all of your pains when it comes to work-life balance, or work-life integration as I like to call it. It's nuanced and definitely not for everyone. What I am suggesting is that by expanding my outlook to be open to more creative opportunities, it let me find ways to embrace and take charge of my circumstances.

> "I NEVER LOSE. EITHER I WIN OR I LEARN."
>
> - NELSON MANDELA

Chapter 6 Exercise

Reflecting on Road Wear

A wise woman in my life talks about *road wear* along one's career or life path. Road wear is her way of saying 'living the lesson where only time, experience, and evolution can teach someone.' It's a concept that we learn best from our own mistakes and experiences.

> "Road wear is living the lesson where only time, experience, and evolution can teach someone."
>
> - Cara Krezek

A wise man in my life, Dr. Barry Wright, who teaches in higher education, challenges his students at the end of a session by asking, "Who are you now? If you are the same person you were an hour ago, you just wasted the hour."

With that in mind, these questions combine road wear with reflection to reveal powerful lessons:

1. Think of a time when you've felt like you compromised, sacrificed, were broken, or lost. In hindsight, what benefits

can you see from that circumstance now?

2. How have you become a better, more resilient person because of it?

Lessons like these aren't just valuable; they're part of what makes you special.

In Japanese culture, there is a practice known as Kintsugi. When a precious piece of pottery is broken or damaged, it is repaired with an adhesive made of gold powder or another precious metal. It's an art form that embraces what is traditionally viewed as damaged or flawed, and turns it into something beautiful.

Reflection Questions:

1. What lessons or insights would you pass along to someone walking the same path? Or to yourself if ever faced with a similar situation?
2. How can this help you evaluate risks when making decisions?

Bonus resources and worksheets are available at: ***www.bestdayeverbook.com/bonus***

"Leadership happens at all levels."

- Jessica Potts

7.

Fitting In And Standing Out

How will I help others belong?

Chapter Purpose:

We can likely all relate to the feeling of being an outsider - it's often uncomfortable and lonely. When you feel disconnected, it isn't easy to feel productive and of value. It's even more difficult to feel engaged and enthusiastic.

This chapter's exercise is about understanding and leveraging your unique way of building trust to foster a sense of belonging and community. It's about fast-forwarding through the discomfort to feel connected to the people you've chosen to surround yourself with. Whether you are a rookie or a veteran on your team, this chapter is about deepening those meaningful connections and relationships to achieve collective goals and feel accepted and appreciated: fitting in while standing out.

When I left my steady government job and launched my own business, I knew that there would be a shift in my social outlets. I had loved the dynamic office environment where interactions - accidental and on-purpose - were part of the day-to-day. There is something special about feeling like part of a team with a higher purpose. While my anchor client provided a place I could belong, I craved something more that I could take on a larger role in growing and shaping.

Teaching at the post-secondary level was something I had dreamed of doing for several years. I didn't have formal training for that, but I did have 10 years of "road wear and reflection." But leading seminars and delivering presentations in my previous role, combined with my enthusiasm for the subject matter, candour, and ability to relate to the emerging generation, had prepared me well.

When I started teaching part-time in the School of Business at the local college, it was a dream come true. I felt confident that I was providing value. And my students responded by nominating me for an Excellence in Teaching Award after my first semester on the job. I didn't win the award, but the real honour is being recognized by the students I spent those 15 weeks with. The experience changed me and likely wouldn't have happened if I hadn't launched my own business.

Thanks to my students' feedback, I was starting to appreciate talents I had that I hadn't appreciated before. They talked about how my class was a safe space where they felt valued and could contribute their opinions openly. I realized that I really enjoyed bringing together a group of misfits and building a community; it was a passion being fulfilled. I was starting to study teamwork and collaboration at the time and could connect the students' feedback to the fundamentals of developing trust and team-building concepts.

I came to look forward to summer term the most - that's when my favourite misfits tended to gather in one glorious semester. Students who take courses over the summer tend to be the ones who start late in the winter instead of the traditional fall start. Typically that means a group of students with the wisdom that experience brings. They show the early signs of road wear.

Some have been dealt personal setbacks that required an extra semester to make up. Some are mature students, young parents, injured workers, or people just seeking to improve their current circumstances. Many are international students who bring worldly and cultural insights. All tended to bring a unique perspective that we can learn from.

The summer of my fourth year of teaching part-time, I was blessed with the most diverse group I had ever had. This group was like a mini United Nations summit with 32 students representing 14 countries, spanning the globe - north, south, east and west. In addition to an outstanding roster of students, the subject was my favourite. The course was called 'Sales & Success Fundamentals'. It wasn't about technical selling, but rather about selling yourself, and other lessons based on traditional soft skills. The table was set for something special.

We were nearing the end of a very memorable semester when the week's topic was "Negotiating Skills and Body Language." The format of each class was the same: I'd start with a TFTD (thought for the day), as my college mentor had done, in the form of a thought-provoking quote related to the topic. We'd share opinions and dialogue about the quotes while challenging our perspectives. A group of students would present on the topic, and then we'd have a break and finish with a guest speaker or an activity and a debriefing.

On this particular day, I came to a realization during the break. As we prepared to transition into the "body language" portion of the session, it dawned on me that my content was based exclusively on North American customs. I knew I needed to adjust my plan quickly since there were only a few minutes left on the break.

Until recently, I had always operated with the Golden Rule in mind:

Treat others how you want to be treated.

The problem was, if I was to treat my students the way I want to be treated with this planned lesson, I might unintentionally do the exact opposite. For example, I was prepared to speak about eye contact as a means of showing respect. But when I looked around the room at my Middle Eastern, Asian, and South Asian students, I realized that eye contact could actually be a sign of disrespect in their cultures. I appreciated at that moment that we had an opportunity to learn and grow and share together.

> "ALONE WE ARE SMART, TOGETHER WE ARE BRILLIANT."
>
> - STEVEN ANDERSON

Knowing that I had built up enough trust for the group to give me the benefit of the doubt for going off-script, I started the second half of the class by confessing my change of plan. Instead of diving into my lesson, I grabbed a stack of sticky notes from my purse (always be prepared!) and handed them out, one to each student, and asked them to write their name on it. In the hallway directly outside of our classroom was a wall-to-wall map of the world. We all moved to the map, and each student placed their sticky note on the corner of the world they called home.

It was a magic moment: a visual representation of the diversity in the room and an opportunity to bring people together by making their voices heard, valued and accepted. After pausing for a photo opp, we went back into the classroom and discussed our cultures and customs in a very open, warm environment.

I brought back my planned lesson, but now we looked at customs in the context of culture. From the meaning of eye contact in North America and the cheek-kissing greetings in Brazil, to bowing in India or showing reverence towards elders, we talked about different types of greetings and the meaning behind each. Every student had an opportunity to be heard and contribute. There were no wrong answers, just an openness and genuine interest in learning from each other. Building trust, respect, and understanding while talking about building trust, respect and understanding.

The flaw with the golden rule became clear. Treating others how *you* want to be treated with the best intentions could still be isolating to people. This solidified in my mind that the Golden Rule is great, but the Platinum Rule is better:

Treat others how they want to be treated.

- By bringing empathy into our experiences.
- By being genuinely curious.
- By allowing people to be heard.
- By recognizing what is special and unique about others.
- By showing acceptance and the absence of judgement.
- By helping others to be understood and to be valued.
- By helping others belong.

By doing this, we not only create a community to belong to, we also help ourselves accept and appreciate who we are.

The next life-changing question presented itself:

How will I help others belong?

I firmly believe that leadership happens at all levels. The responsibility of helping others belong doesn't just fall on the shoulders of the leader. It's the duty of all team members to actively contribute to a sense of belonging. That can be as simple as a smile, a warm welcome, or a simple and sincere compliment. Those are gateway behaviours to deeper connections. And it's essential to recognize that we are part of a team anytime we unite with others in a common experience.

Here are some examples to underscore the importance of belonging.

In 2018, the United Kingdom introduced a Ministry of Loneliness. On the surface that may have sounded silly at the time, but there is a massive business case for promoting human connection. Studies have shown that without it, humans have issues with sleep, symptoms of depression and an increased need for access to health care.

Not only is loneliness – the perceived sense of isolation – costly to our health, it's also costly to our happiness. In 2017, Harvard released a study more than 75 years in the making – the longest study on leading healthy, happy lives. In the report's accompanying TedTalk, Robert Waldinger noted "Loneliness kills. It's as powerful as smoking or alcoholism."

The study credits close relationships with the best predictor of one's happiness: "Those ties protect people from life's discontents, help to delay mental and physical decline, and are better predictors of long and happy lives than social class, IQ, or even genes." *Mineo, Liz. "Good genes are nice, but joy is better." The Harvard Gazette, news.harvard.edu/gazette/story/2017/04/over-nearly-80-years-harvard-study-has-been-showing-how-to-live-a-healthy-and-happy-life. Accessed 11 April, 2017.*

This has never been more apparent than during the global pandemic of 2020. Requisite self-isolation measures and social distancing have punctuated our need for close relationships. As life as I knew it unravelled before me, it was belonging to a writing group that kept me feeling whole. This group of abundant-minded speakers, coaches, educators, and trainers met every weekday morning. It kept me grounded while giving me a reason to get out of bed.

It can be scary being new to a group, but this was a group of coaches, speakers, and people developers who live this philosophy of inclusion, belonging and abundance, so it was easier. We formed a bond through a shared experience that brought us together like a successful round of speed dating. We were individual contributors, each creating our own work for our own businesses and our own reasons. There was no requirement to attend every single day, but many would still advise the group when they would be absent.

An active private social media group and high attendance in regular informal bonus sessions showed me that a sense of belonging breeds both accountability and engagement.

Study after study shows how engagement in the workplace leads to a healthier bottom line. It starts with a psychological commitment and positive regard for how you can provide and exchange value. It isn't just the key to high performance, productivity, and innovation. It's the key to happiness, contentment and fulfillment, and to living your best day ever every day.

Chapter 7 Exercise

Being a Great Team Member

Download a copy of the Building & Maintaining Positive (Working) Relationships checklist from: ***www.bestdayeverbook.com/bonus***

1. What are the traits that make *you* a great team member and help people belong? What can/do people count on you for?
2. Circle or highlight two or three techniques from the checklist that you do most naturally.
3. How do those techniques help you build trust?
4. How do those techniques help you foster a sense of belonging?

Reflection Questions:

1. Think of a team member you've worked with who has had a positive impact on you. Describe what that person did to make you feel that way.
2. (Re)connect with them to tell them how they have impacted or influenced you.

Bonus resources and worksheets are available at: ***www.bestdayeverbook.com/bonus***

"Channel frustration to innovation."

- Jessica Potts

8.

Flipside of Frustrations

What do my pet peeves reveal about my talent?

Chapter Purpose:

In an earlier chapter, we talked about how easy it is to take your talents for granted. Even once you are aware of your talents and strengths, it can be easy to forget how they affect you, even in the simplest circumstances and smallest interactions. That can leave us feeling frustrated and dissatisfied, often without understanding why.

This chapter's exercise is about acknowledging our pet peeves. Those recurring frustrations and minor annoyances we experience in life and using them as clues to reveal and punctuate our values and talents. Whoever thought that being annoyed could be flipped into awareness, appreciation, and application?

By identifying the source behind our triggers, we can begin to reinforce and appreciate who we are, what makes us so special, and channel our awesomeness positively and productively.

It wasn't long ago that I found myself in a simple, everyday situation that revealed I had forgotten about my own talents and found myself feeling frustrated.

Remember how earlier I mentioned that we sometimes mistake our talents for personality quirks? Disregarding compliments we receive when we should be using them as clues to our talents? Likewise, we can learn a lot from examining the things that annoy us – our pet peeves and frustrations.

I'm weird (unique) in my own special ways, as we all are. My most jarring, recurring nightmare is about running late with no way to connect, communicate, or be prepared in various circumstances. I've learned that I am wired for efficiency. So it stands to reason that one of my pet peeves involves time and the inefficient use of it.

There's a clue as to why in my professional life. Earlier, I asked you to think of a time when you felt productive, successful, and of value. Something I've been complimented on – a consistent area of excellence as identified by my peers, and a strength in Gallup's glossary – is the way I facilitate the meetings and sessions I host. I'm known for carefully managing and respecting participants' time by starting and ending on time or asking for consensus to extend the meeting when warranted. Keeping things on schedule and communicating are the same two themes from my recurring nightmare.

The same way we sometimes mistake our talents for personality quirks, we often disregard those compliments we receive when we should be using them as clues to our talents. Likewise, we can learn a lot from examining the things that annoy us.

A few years ago, I found myself feeling annoyed by a particularly inefficient process in my personal life. A process that would often result in consistently being late – or later than planned, which is basically the same thing when you are the person having nightmares about being late! This annoying process is now known as the *"Friday Night Doggy Digestion Dilemma."*

To illustrate the importance of working hard to maintain your awesomeness once you've found it, I'd like to introduce my dog, Dixie. She is a 125lb Great Dane who thinks she is a lap dog. On any given night of socializing, my partner Brent had a habit of doing things in a routine 6-step process as we prepared:

1. Shower.
2. Get dressed.
3. Feed the dog.
4. Wait for the dog to digest.
5. Let the dog out.
6. Give the dog a treat to satiate the guilt for going out.

Total process time: approximately 30 mins.

Now, if you're reading this and you're wired for efficiency like me, you may already be feeling the same sense of frustration. If not, I'll let you in. By the time he was dressed, we were typically already running tight for time, and I'd be turning the corner from annoyed towards frustrated. I'd wonder why he wouldn't just tweak the sequence and feed the dog *before* showering to allow the required time for digestion to happen concurrently, rather than consecutively, and shave 10 mins off prep time.

Total process time: approximately 20 mins.

The same 6-step process rearranged slightly would increase productivity by 33%. And it felt so obvious to me that I expressed it. Brent's calm response was both wise and insightful:

"Not everyone thinks like you."

I was humbled at the realization that I had taken my innate ways of thinking, feeling, and doing – my talent – for granted. Worse, I had let myself become frustrated and a *tad* unpleasant.

The same talent that can help you to be productive (in my case time management) can also contribute to unproductive behaviours. Which leads to our next life-changing question:

What do your pet peeves and frustrations reveal about your talent or values?

We need to pay attention to how we feel. Often, emotional reactions are clues to a place in our lives where we aren't healed from past negative experiences. We need to take action intentionally; otherwise, we find ourselves less effective in our interactions and lives.

Frustration is a feeling; an emotional response triggered when something gets in the way of fulfilling our will, needs, or goals. It can include feeling as though your opinions or efforts aren't appreciated. It's not just minor frustrations that reveal these hidden clues. If something is triggering a sense of frustration, there are two important implications:

1. A frustrated reaction is connected to an emotional response that you have the power to control. You are choosing to perceive a situation in a manner that creates that feeling. What if we choose empathy? Gave the benefit of the doubt? Actively worked to create a scenario where we lead with compassion and empathy instead of frustration? I think of the story of "The Man on the Subway" from Stephen Covey's "Seven Habits of Highly Effective People" when a man gets on a train with his children and disregards their obviously disruptive behaviour. When it's revealed that the man was in shock and en route home from the hospital where his wife had just passed, Covey describes a paradigm shift where his irritation vanished and his heart filled with love and compassion.
2. If you are feeling frustrated, then you aren't feeling happy. And don't we all just want to be happy, content, and fulfilled? By allowing ourselves to feel frustrated without an objective, productive lens, we give over our power and choice in being happy.

Another concept Covey championed is summed up well in this quote:

> "WE JUDGE OURSELVES BY OUR INTENTIONS. AND OTHERS BY THEIR ACTIONS."
>
> - STEPHEN COVEY

What if we started looking for people's good intentions instead of judging them by actions that frustrate us? I think back to a time when I was on the judging end of someone's actions and lived to deeply regret it.

I had become involved in an informal organization that had found success. They recognized that in order to sustain the success they needed to formalize processes and create systems, and it was in my hands. Leading up to the first formal stakeholder meeting, I familiarized myself with the players and their roles. There were many big personalities and egos, as with many organizations, including my own as you'll soon see.

On the night of the first meeting, I felt informed, prepared, and confident in the agenda I had designed. We had carefully polled the group in advance to ensure everyone could attend the first meeting. As people arrived, I got to put faces to the names of the people I had been corresponding with. Only two people were missing as the meeting's start time came and passed.

I don't believe in penalizing the people who arrived on time by delaying the start of meetings to accommodate late-comers, especially when they haven't communicated their delay. This links directly to my efficiency talent/hot-button. We gave the two missing young ladies a few minutes grace before starting introductions. We were about halfway around the table when they burst through the meeting room doors, without pausing their raucous conversation from the hallway, and carrying take-out bags from the adjoining restaurant. They appeared to be slightly intoxicated.

I saw red. I was both frustrated and furious. And I judged them immediately as two people who didn't take this, or themselves, seriously. Additionally, the chip I wore on my shoulder, representing the plight of the young female in the business world, bubbled within. They were making the collective 'us' look bad. I tried to veil my frustration and carry on with the meeting, but inside I had a lot of trouble shaking the contempt I felt toward my contemporaries.

That contempt and judgment from our first meeting carried on throughout our next few interactions. When the leader of the two, Janelle didn't respond or act quickly enough, I refused to give the benefit of the doubt. I found myself looking for reasons to dislike or distrust her, which worked against my goal for contributing to the long-term sustained success of the organization.

Mistake number two came in the form of a realization months later. Things within the organization were in turmoil largely because of the unbecoming, and at times unethical, actions of one of the leaders, which were being exposed as I wound down my contract. My path would cross Janelle's again through a mutual contact, and we sat down for a casual tea months later.

Sure enough, as we found common ground, the conversation pivoted to the organization. She opened up and divulged that a member of the organization, a married man whose own daughters were her age, had made several inappropriate comments and unwanted invitations towards her.

"That's why I was late and tipsy at the first meeting. I just knew I'd need to take the edge off to be in the same room as him." she'd say.

Instantly I knew my error and regretted many decisions about how I had judged and behaved towards her. My lack of awareness and control around my talent and values-born pet peeves and frustration had worked against me. I robbed myself of an opportunity to support and reinforce one of my own values around raising the profile and partnerships of emerging female leaders. I had had what Covey called a paradigm shift, or what Oprah calls an "aha moment".

I've studied innovation, and my favourite definition comes from Canadian commentator Amanda Lang: "Innovation is when a new idea beats an old idea and something changes." I believe that we need to apply this type of frustration innovation to ourselves in order to evolve, grow, and be the most effective and happy people we can be. We need to proactively design our lives in ways that work for us. There is opportunity hidden in frustration. It is an opportunity for innovation with ourselves, our goals, and the people we serve.

> "INNOVATION IS WHEN A NEW IDEA BEATS AN OLD IDEA AND SOMETHING CHANGES."
>
> - AMANDA LANG

Chapter 8 Exercise

From Frustration to Innovation

1. Pay attention to the times you feel frustrated or find yourself ready to vocalize a complaint. This is one of your hot buttons or pet peeves.
2. Dig deeper. What is it about that circumstance, scenario, or person that brings out the emotional reaction in you? If you get stuck, look for clues in your answer to question #3 below.
3. How does your example frustration connect to your values, beliefs, and talents? Check back on your answers in Chapters 1 and 5.

Reflection Questions:

1. Does this exercise reveal any blind spots for you?
2. Once you are aware of the blind spot (a circumstance that gives you an emotional reaction and/or situation that drains your energy), can you challenge yourself to see different perspectives and become more effective and productive?
3. Look at your example frustration. Do your actions align with your broader intentions?

Bonus resources and worksheets are available at: ***www.bestdayeverbook.com/bonus***

"Saying no gives us permission to pursue our yesses with all of our heart and soul."

- Jessica Potts

9.

Niche Priorities

What will I say no to?

Chapter Purpose:

Many of us feel overwhelmed at times, often because we are spread too thin, which keeps us from enjoying life to the fullest. We often have many competing priorities that leave us feeling drained and exhausted.

This chapter's exercise is about focusing on your niche - that area where you can channel your energy for maximum return on investment. More importantly, you will learn to identify the many things that add to the noise and drain your internal resources. You will figure out what you can say *no* to (through re-prioritizing and delegating) in order to say *yes* to the things that bring you positive energy and ignite your inner fire.

When I was establishing my career in my 20s, I said yes to *everything* (not really, but it sure felt like it!). I did that because I had ambition, but not much else in the way of connections or direction.

Saying yes helped me build a network and build a name for myself. But things changed in my 30s with the addition of two active kids — plus my growing business and community involvement. I had as much time as I had always had, but now I had competing priorities. I realized that I had more goals than I had runway left in my life. So eventually, it comes time to choose. My next life changing-question was:

What will I say no to?

Clarity about my goals forced me to assess the value of my time and where to spend it. Not to spoil the ending, but my priorities towards growth have really paid off. With patience and hard work, every time I've said no, an even bigger opportunity has presented itself. Here are some examples:

I mentioned earlier one of my big goals in leaving a safe government job was to teach at the local community college. I had experience in leading seminars and emceeing events. I was comfortable in front of audiences, and helping people develop their dreams made me feel energized. A colleague and I leveraged a community connection to pitch an idea for a new course to the Dean of Business. That meeting opened the door to a teaching gig, which would kickstart my involvement in the more formal side of training and development and bridge my transition to self-employment.

I taught at a school of business and management for about five years and it was gratifying. I loved the environment, and most of all, I loved my students. I knew I had made an impact on them and felt valued. But it took a lot of time to do the job well with my whole heart. With the growing demands of my business, I had to make some tough choices. So, to grow and keep moving towards my evolving goals, I said no to something I loved.

I'm still teaching, but now it's leadership and soft skills development in my own company, and an occasional gig in the professional development arm of the local University's School of Business. I've reflected enough on my humble success to know that it's my soft skills and leadership skills that have led me to where I am. I'm even working on a research project with another arm of the university. I'm not an academic, and in the past, this would have made me feel like an imposter. Today, I can sit in a room with those people who have worked hard for the initials after their names and feel like a peer. I feel like I have value to offer and that I am valued for what I bring.

Around the same time I said no to my beloved teaching role at the college, I also said no to the business group that had been so important in establishing myself in my early career. I used the newfound time and energy to immerse myself in the community of my speaking practice. I joined the Canadian Association of Professional Speakers – C.A.P.S. Oh, how I struggled to see my value there. I've never felt more out of my league than I did at my first few meetings - this was the room of seasoned veterans hitting home runs that I mentioned in the prologue. Olympic gold medalists, former pro sports heroes, titans of business, a soldier, a real estate mogul, doctors, lawyers, all seriously decorated human beings. I left my safe harbour for another round of inferiority complex, but this time I had a plan to leverage my strengths and a positive attitude with this group - and it worked!

I knew that to find value in the group, I had to make meaningful connections with my fellow members. As outgoing as I can be, I felt awkward sitting at a table and making small talk. As the new kid, I had trouble feeling confident in my exchanges. But when I volunteered at the registration desk, I saw my role as making people feel as welcome as possible, like they belonged. Now that was something I could feel confident in doing!

Saying no to my local business group ultimately led to growth and opportunities I had never dreamed possible. In this case, I was elected to the Board of Directors for the largest chapter of C.A.P.S. in the country. It was competitive, and I had never stood for election for anything, ever.

Success seemed to find me, all because I dared to say no for the sake of growth and opportunity.

More recently, the time spent focusing on my business has been really paying off - a series of big gigs meant it was time to hire an administrative helper to grow the business. This wouldn't be the first time I had to take on a team member, but I hadn't had much success with filling the role.

My dad started teasing me, calling me "Murphy Brown," a reference to a 1980s sitcom where the female leader had a revolving door of secretaries over the show's 10 seasons. In my case, I'd had three co-pilots in two years. Whose fault was that? 100% mine!

As I prepared to bring another person into my business life, I wanted to be sure I communicated expectations clearly while also creating clear boundaries around my role. I am the person who wants to do it all but needs to let go. I have struggled with handing over tasks and responsibilities - also known as delegating. That's partly the result of recovering from control freakiness and also because of my deep belief in matching people's talents to tasks.

If I perceived that someone wouldn't thrive in the task because they didn't have the required skill or enthusiasm, I'd hang on to it at a cost to my own outcomes and goals. This creeps up from remnants of my people-pleasing persona.

The result of the exercise was the creation of a solid job description for my new team member that really got to the heart of the role. I also created a job description for myself, which included the four main functions of my position so I could get really clear about my measure of success. It was one of the best time investments I've ever made.

I started tracking tasks and clarifying priorities in three categories to help me say no:

1. **Optimized:** Tasks that you did/plan to do and that you should be doing. This is your sweet spot - the thing that you and your role are made to do that make you feel energized and alive. This is where your time, strengths, goals, and projects align.
2. **Wasted Talent**: Tasks that you did/plan to do and that you shouldn't be doing. These tasks drain energy and resources from your sweet spot tasks. Maybe they are essential tasks to your organization or household, but the task could be done by someone who was properly trained/oriented.
3. **Missed Opportunity**: Tasks that you didn't do and that you should be doing. This area represents missed opportunities, and often requires reflection/connection to broader goals and best practices. This is the important-but-not-urgent box that often starts with, "Ooooh interesting! I'll look at that when things slow down." When you think of the habits of people to whom you aspire to be like, what are you *not* doing?

Once completed, the analysis was clear. I spent a lot of time doing tasks that I shouldn't be doing based on my role and aspirations. My actions weren't aligned with my intended goals and dreams.

This was useful for creating job descriptions and can be used in any scenario where you feel drained or spread thin or aren't getting the results you desire. This same process can work for tasks around the house, in volunteer settings, or anywhere that you have a lead or contributing role.

For me, this exercise brought more freedom and permission to focus on my goals:

1. Clarity with how I should be spending my time;
2. Confidence in bringing my best to my areas of focus;
3. Courage to delegate and hold us all accountable to our roles.

Why? Everyone needs to understand their role, and one of the most important functions of a leader is clarifying and managing expectations of their teammates. Whether leading a household, business, community project, or little league team, everything works better when roles are defined. What's just as important is that the leader has clarity in their role. It can be easy to take on too much and get overwhelmed or be spread too thin to be effective. That leads to stress, sickness, and burnout.

While my practical example is from the business world, I want you to think about this example: You are coaching a children's soccer team. As the leader, you spend time not only developing your team's skills but also helping them understand the rules and roles of the game. We teach them how to be a striker, mid-fielder, defender or goaltender. We encourage everyone to stay in their position so they don't end up chasing a ball like a swarm of bees chasing a rolling flower.

If the coach were to run onto the field and start kicking the ball, the referee would call a foul. The coach's role is expressly to stay off the field during regular play. If the coach doesn't, the team would be punished and the game could be lost.

Sports make this example easy because expectations are clear. There are widely accepted rules that tell everyone what to do and what not to do while outlining the consequences (positive and negative) for all scenarios. Unfortunately, life doesn't have the same playbook, but we can still apply these lessons in the context of our own lives to get the desired results.

Warren Buffet talks about how the most successful people say no to almost everything because those people know how to maximize their time, energy, resources, and impact. We have to learn to say *no* so that we have the resources to commit when it's time for a *yes!* Saying no gives us permission to pursue our yesses with all of our heart and soul. This leads to growth and allows us to evolve into the person we want to be on purpose.

> "THE DIFFERENCE BETWEEN SUCCESSFUL PEOPLE AND REALLY SUCCESSFUL PEOPLE IS THAT REALLY SUCCESSFUL PEOPLE SAY NO TO ALMOST EVERYTHING."
>
> - WARREN BUFFET

Chapter 9 Exercise

Tracking Tasks & Clarifying Priorities

Download a copy of the Tracking Tasks & Clarifying Priorities worksheet from ***www.bestdayeverbook.com/bonus***

When I do this exercise, I maintain accountability by recreating the worksheet on a large flip chart page in my workspace, then add sticky notes with each task.

Steps:

1. Do this daily for 1–2 weeks.
2. Make note of all of the tasks that you complete or aspire to complete each day.
3. Assign each task to a space on the worksheet that corresponds to one of the categories outlined earlier in this chapter. Note that an additional "Optimized" space has been added to record and celebrate the things you said no to.
4. Add the 'extra little tasks' that pop up from emails or other requests where the effort is easy to take for granted.
5. Review, analyse, and evaluate the results.

Tracking Tasks & Clarifying Priorities Categories

	Should Do	Shouldn't Do
Doing	OPTIMIZED :) ***Tasks that you did/plan to do + you should be doing.*** This is your sweet spot - the thing that you and your role are made to do that make you feel energized and alive. This is where your time, strengths, goals, and projects align.	WASTED TALENT X ***Tasks that you did/plan to do + you shouldn't be doing.*** These tasks drain energy and resources from your sweet spot tasks. Maybe they are essential tasks to your organization or household, but the task could be done by someone who was properly trained/oriented.
Not Doing	MISSED OPPORTUNITIES ? ***Tasks that you didn't do + you should be doing.*** This area represents missed opportunities, and often requires reflection/connection to broader goals and best practices. This is the important-but-not-urgent box that often starts with, "Ooh interesting... I'll look at that when things slow down." and are sometimes represented by an email that stays in your inbox 'marked unread'. When you think of the habits of people to whom you aspire to be like, what are you NOT doing?	OPTIMIZED 2.0 :) This is where you delegated or realized something wasn't a priority, so said no.

Reflection Questions:

1. Based on exercise 9, were you surprised to see where most of your time/energy is spent? Why or why not?
2. Pay special attention to the tasks left incomplete, the ones that get bumped from one day to the next:
   a. This may reveal "wasted talent" in a task that doesn't light you up.
   b. Or it may reveal a "missed opportunity" that you didn't make time for - possibly because of other tasks that were more urgent in the moment - but don't necessarily align with your goals or aspirations.
3. What is one thing that you can change today to align your tasks/time to your goals?

Bonus resources and worksheets are available at: ***www.bestdayeverbook.com/bonus***

"Replace 'have to' with 'get to.'"

- Jessica Potts

10.

Blissful Alignment

What am I doing when I have nowhere to be but here and now?

Chapter Purpose:

Picture the quintessential family gathering where a teenager tunes out on their mobile device of choice, disengaged, bored, and wishing they were elsewhere. That's statistically how most people feel about their working lives. They "have" to be there.

This chapter's exercise is our final reflection about how we measure our success and manage our perspectives. Success is about designing a life where we wake up and 'get to' live by having perspective and acceptance about what matters most, and feeling present, engaged, and fulfilled in your life.

Knowing that consistently bringing your best self to the world, and more importantly, how you do that intentionally, is the key to living with no regrets. Trust yourself to make the best decisions and to embrace and accept what life brings.

Years ago, a man named Bob was the peppy speaker at a business breakfast event I attended. His effervescence was infectious as his brand of optimism shone upon us. Bob was the VP of Enthusiasm, and his blood type was B(e)-positive. I'll never forget my shift in perspective when he said, "Become a get-to person in a have-to world." He brought it to life by asking, "Did you get to go to work/school today? Or did you have to go? "

> "BECOME A GET-TO PERSON
> IN A HAVE-TO WORLD."
>
> - BOB KOEHLER

It was my first introduction to a gratitude mindset and the feeling of being engaged in one's life. I'd catch myself and others saying "get to" as another clue to revealing a particular interest or passion. I committed to replacing "have to" with "get to" in all aspects of life. I'd use it as a measurement of where I wanted to spend more time. And as a threshold for when it was time to move on from a project - if I found myself saying or thinking, "I have to..." then I knew it was gut-check time.

I mentioned earlier that I didn't feel like a great mom to my babies. I remember feeling like my kids were at odds with most other aspects of life. I remember one of the grandmas advising that the sooner we accept our role and just surrender to being of service to those little beings, the easier it got. She was right. I feel confident that I am a great mom to my school-aged kids now. I have adopted a lifestyle where work, family, community, and social life all intersect and generally revolve around the kids - my number one priority.

I got it from my mama, who sacrificed a lot for me as a child, and one of her priorities was walking me to school. She had to make special arrangements to align her start time and lunch break at work. With my mom's example, when my kids got to be school age, my new spouse and I made the decision to move into the same neighbourhood as my first husband. We currently live about 25 houses, or a quick bike ride, away from each other, and both houses are walking distance to the kids' school.

A couple of weeks before my 39th birthday, I caught myself thinking that I "have to" walk the dog to pick up the kids at school. Taking a quick inventory of the circumstances, I made the "get to" decision and set out with the dog to collect the kids on that mild Canadian autumn afternoon. I was not disappointed. A magical moment of realization ensued as another life-changing question prepared to present itself.

As I met my kids at the sidewalk outside the school, both greeted me with a hug and handed over their backpacks. I put one on my back and the other on my front, chuckling to myself at how I must've looked: like a pregnant humpback walking a dog nearly big enough to ride. A younger version of myself would've been mortified. Instead, this is how I felt (from a post I made on social media that day):

The glamorous life of the dog-walking, double-backpack-wearing working mom...

In summary: What are you doing when you feel as though there's "nowhere to be but here and now"? And how can you do more of that?

The inspiration: Walking the kids to and from school (with my sidekick Dixie Dane) is one of my very favorite simple things in life. I felt under the weather today but knew this was an important ritual that would bring positive energy, so I made time for it. I'm hardwired to keep a brisk pace when walking (and most other aspects of life!) but something special happened today when the wise words of a friend entered my mind. "BREATHE"

(This friend happens to be a world-class Mixed Martial Arts competitor. We know each other through our work with a community organization, where he serves as a Mental Strength Coach helping 'regular people' do extraordinary things.)

Almost every morning, Mat sends inspiring lessons, quotes, and anecdotes to our group including:

"THERE IS ALWAYS OPPORTUNITY FOR GROWTH IF YOU COMMIT YOURSELF TO REFLECTION AND BREATHING."

- MAT ROCCA

I inhaled deeply as his words echoed in my mind. I exhaled deeply and slowed my stride. I inhaled and felt the sunshine on my face. I exhaled feeling a sense of gratitude and satisfaction. I inhaled and exchanged smiles and waves with a neighbour mowing his lawn.

I exhaled and realized how perfect this moment was. I reflected on how invested and free I felt in that moment "with nowhere to be but here and now."

In that moment, it dawned on me that "nowhere to be but here and now" is, to me, the very definition of being engaged in life, whether work, school, family, community, or any other aspect. It's about making the simple choice to show up and be present – like we "get to" be there. If something is worth your time, it's worth your full attention. We aren't bored teenagers at the holiday dinner table anymore.

Where are you when you feel as though there's "nowhere to be but here and now?"

That's the feeling of a "best day ever." To me, that's the definition of being engaged in life. It's energizing. Know what you want. Want what you've got. Appreciate. Breathe. Simply put: success equals doing more of what you love, with those you love, on purpose. Set yourself up to replace "have to" with "get to."

It was the cumulative experiences you've heard that lead to that perfect moment.

Chapter 10 Exercise

A Final Reflection on Presence and Passion

1. Where are you and what are you doing when you have "nowhere to be but here and now"?
2. What made you excited to get out of bed recently? Why?
3. What do you need to do to replace "have to" with "get to"?
4. How might you do more of what you love?

Bonus resources and worksheets are available at: ***www.bestdayeverbook.com/bonus***

Epilogue

'Perspective'

And then 2020 happened...

With an appreciation for the simple beauty in life, I had found myself in a good place as the calendar turned to 2020 - my 40th year. I've never felt burdened by aging. I've enjoyed growing and pruning my streak of grey hair and watching the laugh lines form around my eyes. I've earned every one of those grey hairs and wrinkles, and I welcome the wisdom they've brought.

So when I sat down with my high school girlfriends to solidify plans for our collective 40th birthday trip overseas, we were setting the table for a big year. We wanted to go somewhere that none of us had ever been - to do something together for the first time.

The idea, impact, and importance of doing something new had been punctuated recently when I ran my first obstacle course-style event with a group of friends. I've never been particularly athletic but found myself surprised by how energizing the experience was. That was the day I embraced John C. Maxwell's quote as a mantra, ***"When was the last time you did something for the first time?"*** There was alignment with one of my favourite lessons about stretching yourself outside of your comfort zone for the sake of growth (reference Chapter 1).

In the days that followed our travel planning meeting, I decided that I would issue a challenge to give myself the greatest gift I could give: the gift of meaningful connection. I called it my #40firsts Project and here's what it looked like:

Challenge:

Help me prove that "Life begins at 40" by letting me experience a slice of your life, and live vicariously through your passions! I'm up for anything, and I want to see you in your element... here are some ideas:

- *Baking biscotti? Sounds great!*
- *Ziplining at Niagara Falls? Yes!*
- *Helping to build a tree fort? Sign me up!*

The fine print...

- *Nothing harmful.*
- *I'll do (just about) anything. But I won't EAT anything.*
- *Nothing that will embarrass or bring shame to my kids.*
- *And most importantly... with YOU!*

What do you love to do? How can we do it together?

In addition to trying new things, my #40firsts Project was about human (re)connection and seeing my people at their best. Several friends - some old and some new - responded with ideas through social media. Within a week, I had a list of more than 40 things to do in 2020. I managed to get 5 "firsts" scheduled and completed within the first six weeks of the project launching in mid-January. With each new activity, I was stretching myself, building and rebuilding bonds of friendship, humbling myself, and trusting in my companion. Laughing, learning, enjoying the process, and looking forward to the next. I was living in a "get to" frame of mind.

Then, in early March, our global pandemic changed the world with self-isolation and social distancing. My plans got put on hold, and I decided to extend my deadline to my 41st birthday in late 2021. #40firsts slowed as the world slowed, but it wasn't forgotten as I added number 6 to the list: enjoying virtual cocktails with travel pals, which was totally new to us at the time. Now we chuckle as the world has been forced to embrace the virtual world in the ensuing months!

It was the 7th edition of #40firsts that would be the most memorable, defining, and life-changing: riding in an ambulance for the first time and wondering if I would ever return home to my family.

Let me rewind to May 31, 2020. It was a Sunday, and it started as a perfect day - the type of day that makes you appreciate the little things. With full bellies and hearts, my family took our newest addition - Penny, a rescue dog who had arrived the day before - for a family walk. Just before 11am, we arrived at the picturesque park surrounded by a small body of water, a place I refer to as my own personal heaven-on-earth.

We enjoyed the onset of summer weather, breezes by the water, birds singing, my happy, active kids picking mini bouquets of newly bloomed wildflowers, and celebrating new beginnings. We paused under a series of willow trees to take a photo of a stunning bird with iridescent feathers. I made a note to send it to my Uncle Bob, the bird watcher, to see what type of bird it was.

This perfect day of simple pleasures made it too easy to ignore the warning signs, including the slight loss of coordination on my left side, chalked up to maybe having slept awkwardly - nothing to be alarmed about. So I downplayed it. Surely, it wasn't worth disrupting this best day ever in progress.

By the time we got home just before noon, I knew it was something that couldn't be ignored. With the grace of a television mom from the 1960s, I sent the kids downstairs to play, then my demeanour changed completely as I whisked my partner upstairs, demanding he do a stroke test. By noon, I had lost all of the function in my left hand. We called a healthcare hotline, who walked us through another stroke test and told us to immediately call an ambulance. An ambulance? No! I didn't want to go to the hospital during COVID-19. I didn't want to go to the hospital at all!

My partner took charge and called the kids' dad, who arrived within moments to whisk them away. There was no point in burdening them with the knowledge that their mom isn't invincible. They were scheduled to go to daddy's in a couple of hours anyway, not due back for about 48 hours — plenty of time for me to sort this out without them knowing.

I tried desperately to persuade my left hand to return to its functional state using an intense "superhero" stare and sheer willpower. Brent and I laughed through the uncertainty, but despite these moments of levity during the initial assessment, I was terrified. At this point, I was feeling my own mortality in a way I had never experienced before. As I reluctantly awaited the ambulance's arrival, my denial of the circumstances was replaced by panic ... I hadn't hugged my kids goodbye.

While it was an emotional moment for me directly, it was the love for my children that compelled me next. It wasn't just the thought of my precious kids growing up without a mom; it was the idea of my sweet boys potentially living with the guilt of not hugging me goodbye. They had already been gone for several minutes, but that didn't stop me from desperately 'running' down the hall in my weakened state to try to catch them. I'm lucky that Brent heard me stumble off the bed because he caught me at the top of the stairs, where I would have fallen.

Within 2 hours of taking the photo of the bird with the beautiful iridescent feathers, I was being wheeled through the hospital on a gurney on route to a CT scan, MRI, and a battery of other tests. Because of the pandemic, Brent wasn't able to ride with me in the ambulance or come to the hospital. I was scared, but felt safe and stable, cracking jokes and making friends with my caregivers. My mom always said you get better service when you smile, and I knew healthcare was no different.

It was the exceptional care of an amazing team of health

professionals who found the lesion on my brain. And the same team who bolstered my spirits when I was at my lowest, loneliest points. My all-inclusive, 3-day, 2-night stay in the local hospital's stroke ward brought more tests, including another MRI and lumbar puncture (spinal tap), which for anyone wondering, was far less painful than childbirth.

What none of these tests brought was a diagnosis. I went home with a stroke exercise kit to rehabilitate the significant loss of fine motor skills and wobbly balance, as well as a will to live with a renewed perspective.

My new outlook wasn't a major shift, but it was an important one. I had been thinking about my friend Dr. Scott, who himself had survived a massive stroke about 5 years earlier. If he had treated his symptoms as flippantly as I had, he wouldn't have survived. Years ago, he shared his stroke story with me and spoke of the moment where he realized that he was free of regret in life. I thought that was a magnificent revelation, and it stuck with me.

To me, having no regrets in the most uncertain moments means you are living fully and purposely with acceptance and hope. And with that perspective, you know the best is still yet to come. When I experienced my own similar circumstance, I had a comparable revelation to Dr. Scott. In those critical moments of facing my own mortality, my only regret in life was not giving my children a hug before departing in the ambulance. Aside from that, I only felt peace and contentment in my life. I was truly living my best day ever every day.

In the coming weeks, the healthcare team ruled out many things, from a brain tumour to infectious diseases to a stroke. Would you believe that my next revelation came through the disappointment I felt when they advised me that it wasn't a stroke? Dr. Scott had come to visit a week or so ahead of the disappointing news, and we rehashed our health scare stories. He had told me about his will and determination to expedite his recovery process by retraining his brain to regain function. Even if that meant the risk of falling and failing, over and over again. I was disappointed because a stroke meant I wouldn't be in control of my own recovery the way Dr. Scott had been.

With the news that it wasn't a stroke, I felt helpless in my recovery. At the same time, the doctor mentioned a potential indication of a rare and aggressive form of Multiple Sclerosis (MS). When I searched the internet, the first description I saw included "rapid onset of paralysis." I closed the browser window and immediately decided to take control of my perspective before my mind had a chance to absorb and manifest back pain in some type of reverse placebo effect.

It was time to take my power back through perspective. In the absence of a specific plan based on a specific diagnosis, I decided to take control of my health the only way I could. I made the choice to eat well, exercise more, rest my body, stress less, and maintain a positive outlook. Those were the things I could control, and it was an empowering shift.

My neurologist now feels comfortable diagnosing it as a one-time event. I feel comfortable calling it an awakening and an affirmation. In the months that have passed since then, I am kinder and gentler than I had been - or "less intense" as my mom would say. I'm excited to continue learning, growing, and evolving knowing that the best is yet to come.

Every day brings us the gift of perspective - an opportunity to choose how we see the world - where we can decide to make today the best day ever.

My final wish for you is simple.

- I wish for you to wake with excitement, poised for the day.
- I wish for you to feel alignment and abundance as you shine your light into the world.
- I wish for you to say "more days like today" with clarity and intention.
- I wish for you to settle into bed feeling fulfilled, valued, and purposeful.
- I wish for you a lifetime of healthy perspective, alignment, and opportunities to make your day a best day ever.